BOOKS AUTHORED BY Emma S. Etuk

1. 2010 A Splendid Ecstasy: The Trials, Thrills & Joys Of Authorship. Bloomington, IN: Authorhouse, Inc.
2. 2010 THE AUDACITY OF FAITH: The Relevance of Faith to Success. New York: iuniverse, Inc.
3. 2008. NEVER AGAIN: Africa's Last Stand. New York: iuniverse, Inc.
4. 2006. THE INDISPENSABLE VISIONARY: Turning Your Dreams Into Realities. Washington, D.C: Emida International Publishers.
5. 2004. RECIPE FOR SUCCESS: The 21 Indispensable Things That Can Help You Succeed in Life. Washington, D.C: Emida International Publishers.
6. 2002. LISTEN AFRICANS: Freedom Is Under Fire. Washington, D.C: Emida International Publishers.
7. 2000. WHAT'S SO GOOD ABOUT CHRISTIANITY? Five Amazing Ways the Gospel Has Influenced and Blessed Our Lives. Washington, D.C: Emida International Publishers.
8. 1999. FRIENDS: WHAT WOULD I DO WITHOUT THEM? Finding Real and Valuable Friendships in an Unfriendly World. Washington, D.C: Emida International Publishers.
9. 1997. FATHERHOOD IS NOT FOR BABIES: Becoming the Kind of Father You Really Want To Be. Washington, D.C: Emida International Publishers.
10. 1996. Co-author, Ethnic and Cultural Diversity in Nigeria. Trenton, NJ: Africa World Press.
11. 1990. A WALK THROUGH THE WILDERNESS. New York: Carlton Press.
12. 1989. DESTINY IS NOT A MATTER OF CHANCE: Essays in Reflection and Contemplation on the Destiny of Blacks. New York: Peter Lang.
13. 1978. GO YE OUT. Uyo, Nigeria: Nigeria For Christ Tracts Ministry.

T0171708

LISTEN AFRICANS!
A REVOLUTION IS COMING

Why It Must Come and How We Should Deal with It

Emma Samuel Etuk

iUniverse, Inc.
Bloomington

Listen Africans! A Revolution Is Coming
Why It Must Come and How We Should Deal with It

iUniverse books may be ordered through booksellers or by contacting:

iUniverse
1663 Liberty Drive
Bloomington, IN 47403
www.iuniverse.com
1-800-Authors (1-800-288-4677)

Because of the dynamic nature of the Internet, any Web addresses or links contained in this book may have changed since publication and may no longer be valid. The views expressed in this work are solely those of the author and do not necessarily reflect the views of the publisher, and the publisher hereby disclaims any responsibility for them.

Any people depicted in stock imagery provided by Thinkstock are models, and such images are being used for illustrative purposes only.

Certain stock imagery © Thinkstock.

ISBN: 978-1-4502-7734-1 (pbk)
ISBN: 978-1-4502-7736-5 (cloth)
ISBN: 978-1-4502-7735-8 (ebk)

Printed in the United States of America

iUniverse rev. date: 1/13/2011

ADVANCE Praise for the Book

A Change is of vital importance in any situation, be it major or minor. In his book, <u>Listen Africans! A Revolution is Coming</u>, [Etuk] explains that a revolution is about a fundamental change to the basic fabric of society.

Based upon the experience of other writers and on his own experience, he has adequately researched into the origin of revolutions and reveals that revolution has its origin from Heaven, where Lucifer (Satan) rebelled against God because he (Satan) wanted to be God, thus emphasizing the fact that one ingredient of revolution is a threat to the status quo.

[Etuk] affirms that not all revolutions are good and not all are bad either, but the motivation for any revolution is of vital importance. He considers the intentions, purposes and irrepressibility or inevitability of revolutions. These considerations make a revolution in Africa a must as he (the writer) addresses Africans.

...the depth of knowledge and information in this book make it a must read.

— Air Vice-Marshall Benjamin Cole (rtd.), Ghana.

Emma Etuk argues that no society can survive for long under conditions of inequality. Otherwise a revolution is unavoidable. In this book, he critically discusses the need for an African revolution and the liberating effect of faith. This is a fascinating read for all Africans who believe in the need for a revolutionary transformation of the continent.

— John O. Davies-Cole, Ph.D., MPH.
Public Health Specialist.

Etuk has been indefatigable in his profound determination for an African Revolution as admonished not only in this piece but [also] in his other books. Indeed he has constantly proclaimed the need for Africans to be proud of their ancient heritage with the deliberate intention of making Africa an inspiration to the entire world. This piece must be read by everyone alive.

— Adams O. Adah, Founder, IMPART AFRICA, Nigeria.

Listen Africans! A Revolution is Coming ... is not just for Africans to listen, but all the nations of the world. Dr. Etuk, in this prophetic sounding of the trumpet call for the impending revolution, writes in the tradition of a zealot and sounds like the political philosopher, Niccolo Machiavelli of the 13th century.

Etuk blends the values of societal structures that have become stagnated into a melting cauldron for revolution. He strategically identifies and draws out of the wells of past heroes of revolution to get his readership look to the past as evidential proofs that history will always repeat itself. He identifies a couple of revolutionaries and challenges us to draw our inspiration from [them].

But like most exponents of past revolutions in our checkered African history, Dr. Etuk sues for quiet and non-militant ... revolution. I, therefore, recommend this text as a literature and social science material.

— Sam U. Imong, [ABD]
Logos Global Networks,
Jacksonville, Florida.

This book is dedicated to the late irrepressible social crusader,
Chief GANI FAWEHINMI,
And all the Freedom Fighters of our generation.

ACKNOWLEDGMENTS

As always, I begin by giving all the honor, praise and glory to God, the Lord of all creation, for the wisdom and knowledge to put ideas to paper for the blessing of mankind. I could not have written all these books without His help. He must be pre-eminent in all that we do, since we owe Him our very lives.

I wish to thank all those who have been my financial backers during the execution of each project. Some have caused me tears of joy when I observe that they give to my writing career out of need. To Dr. Onu and Tayo, and their families, I will ever be grateful. They give beyond their capabilities because they believe in the power and impact of the written word.

Next, I wish to thank those who take the time to read the manuscript before it is sent to production. No one writer is absolutely perfect and thorough in his or her work. We need the searching eyes of our peers and this is needful in the art of writing. These are my proof-readers and advisers, the blurb-writers.

In this respect, I wish to thank Air Vice Marshall Benjamin Cole, who was the first to show appreciation for this work and to believe in it. Also, I thank my precious friend, Adams O. Adah, of IMPART Africa; Dr. Sam U. Imong, the irrepressible student in his quest for knowledge and excellence; Dr. John O. Davies-Cole, a Public Health Specialist, and Dr. Sulayman Nyang, my intellectual mentor.

I wish to thank the Church of the Living God, Forestville, Maryland, and Pastor, Reverend Dr. Stephen K. Gyermeh, who has supported my writings in all the years that I have been a member of that church. Indeed, I am and will always, be grateful to them.

Lastly, but not the least, I am grateful to members of my immediate family, by whom God has given to me the responsibility of oversight and the hard role of leadership. Many a times, I pray for mercy because I feel not to qualify for this job. But the thought of having a family is, indeed, a precious, human feeling and thought. To God be all the glory for seeing me through the authorship of my thirteenth book. I covet the earnest prayers of all my friends and well-wishers.

CONTENTS

FOREWORD

Dr. Etuk has spent a great deal of time and attention to the idea of revolution. In doing so, he read widely on the literature. He check[ed] what the leading students of the subject said about the matter and he made the effort to relate these texts to the African contexts, which are the driving factors for his analysis and commentaries.

In looking into the question of revolution and its historical manifestations, Etuk, who has written so far more than a dozen books on matters relating to Africa and other aspects of the human condition, seized the opportunity to tell his readers the etymological origins of the term and the manner in which peoples from the West have been affected by the movement of this term from one region of conceptualization to the other.

Knowing fully well that the idea and the term existed among students of physics and astronomy, he developed an argument ostensibly to demonstrate how the term revolution captures a variety of ideas and understanding among many of us in the modern world. While developing his ideas, [Etuk] revealed to us how any documentation of the idea of revolution in Africa will be lacking if the story of imperialism and colonialism are not fully examined and critically evaluated.

Etuk revisited the conquest by the Portuguese through their development of the caravels and what followed soon after their conquest. Tracing the modern plight of the African peoples to the 545 years of European hegemony and domination, Dr. Etuk reminds us about the military, political, economic, and cultural consequences for the African people. Not only were persons of African descent captured and sold as slaves through the Middle Passage, but they were effectively emasculated and trafficked as Black Cargo for the gratification of the conquering Europeans.

What's striking in this narrative is Dr. Etuk's ability to relate the texts on colonialism and imperialism to the struggle for freedom in human society. Drawing conclusions from the Western narratives about freedom and the quest for justice in Western societies, Etuk found a gateway to analysis and affirms how, when and why the idea of revolution in Africa, which to some is not overdue, deserves immediate attention.

In order to make his point categorically clear, Etuk reminds all of us that revolution is a universal phenomenon and the African Revolution, which is making headway into the minds and dreams of many black men and women, is part of that universal phenomenon.

Etuk returns our train of thought to the European narratives and on how their stories relate to the African Story. It is as a result of this study and analysis that Dr. Etuk comes to the identification and analysis of five revolutions of the last two centuries. They are the British Glorious Revolution, the American Revolution, the French Revolution, the Russian Revolution, and the Chinese Revolution.

Taking each of these revolutions, Etuk analyzed the available narratives to make his point about human hostility to oppression and injustice. By telling the stories of the English people who lamented the tragedy of King Charles I, and the events leading to his collapse, Etuk showed us how power corrupts and in doing so, conditions leading to a revolution often comes into being.

Etuk links the tale of two cities, as Charles Dickens effectively captured in his analysis of revolution in France, and the Nigerian scholar moves on to demonstrate how the two revolutions emerged out of the weaknesses of the powerful and growing pains and agony of the ruled. This spirit of ventilation of the climate of opinion in the societies, affected by the spirit of revolution, came out loud and clear in his telling of the French Revolution.

As is now commonly known in the literature, the French Queen to King Louis XVI of France apparently failed to garner sufficient subtleties on how to live and act French because of her Austrian feelings of superior and political arrogance. As a result of this state of affairs, Dr. Etuk tells us, not only did the king lose power but the train of events eventually led to his execution.

The French people were doomed to witness bloodshed in the most horrible ways and the Guillotine was destined to the name of a person whose descendants were too embarrassed and frightened to carry the name. Another anecdote was the widely quoted statement attributed to Queen Marie Antoinette: "Let them eat cake," an insulting statement whose reverberation would differentiate the nature of political violence in France and the consequences for the British and French systems of government in the running of their affairs.

Etuk tells us what happened in England and France, but he also examined the writings of the scholars working in these fields of study. At the end of his story-telling and analysis, Etuk identified the forces and factors contributing to what happened during the French Revolution. The messages and lessons from these struggles were catalogued ostensibly to tell Africans that their stories could be analogies to what happened in Europe.

Not only did Etuk say so: he also led his readers on to the Russian Revolution and the Chinese Revolution. In telling the stories of the Russian and the Chinese, Etuk gave us background information on the cast of characters whose activism and thoughts propelled the call for revolution.

Reading Dr. Etuk's book would give his readers a distillation of what has been collected by other scholars and, in doing so, adds to the African quest for meaning in this life where revolutions are present, here and there, but still strange in the thoughts and imaginations of African people. Etuk builds on the time of his thinking and tells us about Marx, Lenin, Engels, and others whose activism led to the overthrow of the Czar and his nobility.

Writing about the Chinese Revolution, Dr. Etuk demonstrated how critical political agitation, social mobilization and political propaganda combined in all these struggles for change. Not only do you see the revolution mobilizing the masses in their respective social categories to effect change, but Etuk shows how the peasantry played a bigger role in the Chinese Revolution. By so doing, Etuk reaffirmed the analysis of many scholars who had studied the respective revolutions and identified the convergence and divergence between conflicts.

The Americans, for example, opted for a revolution with a republican dispensation in mind; the British killed their king under Oliver Cromwell, without effecting a republican regime. A counter-revolution took place after the Restoration. Not only did the French duplicate the American republican narrative, but they went to higher levels. They overthrew their king and his nobles and, at the same time, dismantled the Church and installed a new political and psychological dispensation.

What came out loud and clear in Etuk's narratives about the Chinese was the grand struggle led by Mao Tse-tung and the Big March of the Communist Party in China in the seizing of power at the expense of the Kuomintang, led by Chiang Kai-shek who lost the mainland China, fled to Taiwan where they continue to rule to this day.

A number of questions have come to my mind in the writing of a Foreword to this book. To the readers of this text, I will leave five points to remember about Dr. Etuk's attempt to draw from the global narratives on revolution a source of inspiration for Africans and persons of African descent around the world.

1. The first point is the reality of revolution in human history and the relevance of Dr. Etuk's call for change and action from the African people. He has marshaled the much needed facts for all to see and hear, but he has also brought to our attention the lessons of history. They are there for all to witness.

2. The second point that I wish to raise here is the critical analysis suggested in his book. He tells us that violence is inevitable, but he also warns the African leadership to pay close attention to the arguments of the tyrannically oppressed and their determination to be free and capable to administer their own things.

3. The third point relates to arguments made in this book. Dr. Etuk is familiar with the historical and metaphysical arguments about freedom and justice in human societies. He is firmly committed to the Christian narratives about life and death. And for this and other related reasons, his analysis of revolution covers both the human/historical and the spiritual/transcendent.

There is the hand of God in these narratives because the idea of a revolution originated with the rebellion of Satan against the Divine Order. To Dr. Etuk, life is an event that could be properly harnessed by those who wish well to others in the world and, simultaneously, try consciously to make life better for all without a social or political revolution.

Whenever things change for the worse, and human power is deployed through the manipulation of the state, in the service of those who control it, in Dr. Etuk's view, such forces of evil are cohorts of Satan in the human world.

4. The fourth and fifth points which I wish to share here is that this book of Dr. Etuk is a GPS for those who listen and a familiar voice for those Africans who, in many ways, have committed the great acts of self-denegation through their mortgage of their African identity to foreign cultures and languages.

This is a political, economic and cultural answer to the African call for revolution. For whom the bell tolls; it tolls for all African people and the rainbow above is sending the signals.

Dr. Sulayman S. Nyang,
Professor of African Studies,
Howard University
Washington, D.C.

INTRODUCTION

CHANGE is a word we all are familiar with. But when the more frightening version of it — revolution – is used, we get nervous and apprehensive. We need not be nervous and apprehensive because change is necessary in life. Except, perhaps, for the moon and the sun, everything else in life changes. People change. Governments change. Life itself is full of changes. African life must have changes that are progressive and that lead to prosperity. Change is the other name for revolution. After 545 (1415-1960) years of Europa-African relations, a time when the Africans went through slavery and colonialism, there ought to be a continent-wide re-consideration for revolutionary action.

This book is not the only one calling for change. Chinua Achebe, Africa's most renowned novelist, is said to be calling for a revolution (change) in Nigeria.1 The Lagos-based educationist, Pat Utomi, is another. Ikenna Anokute, a writer in New York city, is quoted as saying: "I believe Nigeria is ripe for a revolution, bloody or preferably peaceful."2

In 2008, "a call was made at a book launch by a bourgeois lawyer and an acclaimed legal scholar, Professor Ben Nwabueze, on the need for a bloody revolution in Nigeria."3 Other names linked to the call for a revolution in Nigeria include the Governor of Lagos State, Babatunde Fashola, Lieutenant-General Theophilus Danjuma, Chief Olisa Agbakoba, the Nigerian Bar Association president, and Chief Orji Kalu, the former Abia State governor.4

What has generated interest for a revolutionary change in Nigeria is also true of the other African countries. There are causes for this outcry for revolution. These include the following:

1. Broken promises made by several post-independence governments
2. Poverty that has reached unbearable proportions
3. Hunger
4. Infrastructural decay
5. Youth unemployment and frustrations
6. Environmental pollutions
7. Kleptocracy and official corruption
8. State-sponsored terrorism and murders
9. Bad governance
10. Myopic and political visionlessness
11. Tyranny and dictatorships
12. Ineffective leadership
13. Ethnic and religious strives and violence, like the Boko Haram crisis, in Nigeria, in which an estimated one thousand people died and three Christian pastors were beheaded
14. Labor unrests and dissatisfaction. The list can go on and on.

In the country of Rwanda, the political and social crises there have been festering and appear to have no end in sight. Kenya, Uganda, and Zimbabwe have witnessed political turbulences. In Zimbabwe, Robert Mugabe has been in power for 30 years (1980-2010) and counting.

Human life in Africa has gotten worse since 1960, the year of Africa's independence from colonial rule. Why? Where are the dividends of the freedom from European colonial rule? Against the above background, the author of this book provides both a historical analysis and an ideological synthesis on the idea of revolution.

This author examines the definition, origin of, and the necessity for an African revolution. The author believes that there is a theological basis for such a continent-wide revolutionary change in Africa. He insists that there are five kinds of revolutions, namely, bloody, peaceable, quiet, ethical and a Jesus revolution. He leaves the responsibility of choice to his readers to decide what kind of revolution Africans should adopt in their efforts to change the continent.

In the end, this writer states that Africans can learn from history's six major revolutions of the past, namely: Hebrew, English, American, French, Russian, and Chinese. They do not have to re-invent the wheel.

He admonishes that the Africans must prepare themselves for the coming, inevitable Revolution.

This is a timely book as Africa begins her journey into the second decade of the 21st century. It is a must-read book, one that must be on the hands of every student, university class-room and library. It is a book which answers the question, "How Can Africans Survive?"

CHAPTER ONE
A Definition For Revolution

The problem associated with the definition of the term, revolution, is similar to that of defining the word pornography, of which it has been said that there is hardly any adequate and satisfactory definition. But when you see it, you know what it is. When a revolution occurs and you see it, you know what it is.

In the past, there have been many attempts to define the word, revolution. But I would like to begin here with Chairman Mao Tse-tung's (1893-1976) often-quoted statement that "a revolution is not a dinner party. It cannot be so kind, so refined."1 Mao went on to say that "a revolution is an insurrection, an act of violence by which one class overthrows another."2

Mao's definition implies that any fundamental change in society resulting from a revolution has to come by the barrels of a gun. Understood in this way, every kind of revolution involves sweat and bloodshed. But even before Mao's definition, other kinds of definitions of revolution existed. We can consider that of the historian, Crane Brinton, whose book, The Anatomy of Revolution, first appeared in 1938 and was republished in 1952 and 1965. It is now a classic.

In his book, Brinton admitted that a "revolution is one of the looser words," but he added that "at one end of the spectrum of the meanings revolution has come in common usage to be hardly more than an emphatic synonym for 'change,' perhaps with a suggestion of sudden or striking change."3 "Obviously in present usage," Brinton

1

wrote, "the word 'revolution' is a class term covering quite a number of concrete phenomena."4

In her book, <u>On Revolution</u> (1963), Hannah Arendt (1906-1975), perhaps the most read author on this subject, examined the principles which underlie all revolutions. She contended that revolutions are not about "mere changes" but are about bringing into existence "something altogether new."5 A revolution, she wrote, is about "a complete change of society," like "the emancipation of the slavish part of all mankind all over the earth."6

In the view of Arendt, the most important element in a revolution is "to change the fabric of society."7 She noted that "all modern revolutions are essentially Christian in origin, and this even when their professed faith is atheism."8 This is interesting since I have contended that the first revolution occurred in heaven where God abides.

Arendt added this statement:

> The modern concept of revolution [is] inextricably bound up with the notion that the course of history suddenly begins anew, that an entirely new story, a story never known or told before, is about to unfold…9

Also, Arendt insisted that "crucial…to any understanding of revolutions in the modern age is that the idea of freedom and the experience of a new beginning should coincide."10 "It is not only our understanding of revolution," she stated, "but our conception of freedom."11 Chapter One of her book, covering 38 pages, is devoted to an analysis of "the Meaning of Revolution."12

Regarding the American Revolution, Arendt observed that "no historian will ever be able to tell the tale of our century without stringing it 'on the thread of revolutions.'"13 It is valuable to add that Arendt provided some insights into the nature of revolutions after her publication of <u>The Origins of Totalitarianism</u>, in 1948. This book was posthumously republished in 1976.

Karl Marx (1818-1883), who was a keen observer of human society and of political changes, also had a definition for revolution. In an analysis provided by Michael Lowy, one of Marx's biographers, Marx described a socialist revolution as a political revolution with a social soul, thus:

Revolution in general – the overthrow of the existing power and dissolution of the old relationships – is a political act . But socialism cannot be realized without revolution. It needs this political act insofar as it needs destruction and dissolution. But where its organizing activity begins, where its proper object, its soul comes to the fore – there socialism throws off the political cloak.14

Hence, for Marx, like with Mao, revolution was primarily about the overthrow, destruction and dissolution of an existing or old socio-political order. It was about the class struggles within a society. The Marxian conception of revolution was fully expressed by the publication of the Communist Manifesto in 1848. The "dictatorship of the proletariat" was the eventful triumph of the class struggles through violence.

In 1971, Dr. Vernon C. Grounds published his book, Revolution and the Christian Faith. The introduction of the book was written by Senator Mark O. Hatfield from the state of Oregon. Dr. Grounds provided different meanings of the word, revolution, including an analysis of the origin of the term. Chapter One of the book is titled, "Total Revolution."

In his book, Dr. Grounds pointed out that the term revolution was originally an astronomical word, "which gained increasing importance in the natural sciences ..." and he added:

> In this scientific usage it retained its precise Latin meaning, designating the regular, lawfully, revolving motion of the stars, which, since it was known to be beyond the influences of man and hence irresistible, was certainly characterized neither by newness nor by violence. On the contrary, the word clearly indicates a recurring, cyclical movement.15

Dr. Grounds then stated that "nothing could be farther from the original meaning of the word ... than the idea of which all revolutionary actors have been possessed and obsessed, namely, that they are agents in a process which spells the definite end of an old order and brings about the birth of a new world."16

I wish, with all my heart, that all current and future revolutionaries kept faith with the original meaning of the term. But, this, in reality, is only a wishful thinking. The association of revolutions with violence and destruction – the Marxian and Mao's conceptions of the term — have come to stay, carrying with them the bloodiness and carnage of modern warfare!

Grounds defined a "literal revolution" as "the deliberate use of terror and violence in an attempt to disrupt, subvert, and destroy the whole established order, replacing it with some new form of government and way of life."17 This phrase, "way of life," is quite significant. For, a coup-de-tat may violently bring forth a new form of government but not necessarily a "new way of life," or a revolution.

Furthermore, Grounds cited one of his former professors at Rutgers University, Everett Dean Martin, author of the book, Farewell to Revolution (1935), in which Martin contended that a revolution is "a social earthquake ... a barbarian invasion and conquest ... the supreme exhibition of mob violence."18 In his reaction to Martin, Grounds contended that a revolution is "a futile tragedy and a tragic futility."19

Dr. Grounds also added that judged by Martin's criterion, "the ten great revolutions of history" constituted "a drama of delusion."20 "Only a moronic sadist," Grounds said, "would dream of fomenting armed insurrection in our day."21

I have already cited the views of Hannah Arendt whose work Dr. Grounds described as "magisterial."22 But Grounds also wrote about Paul Hutchinson, author of the book, World Revolution and Religion (1931) who "saw and foresaw revolution occurring politically, industrially, socially, racially and religiously."23

Going ahead of myself, I believe that it is safe to add here that revolutions can be culturally, intellectually and scientifically understood. After all, Bernard Bailyn, the American intellectual historian, saw the American Revolution as an ideological revolution while Charles Beard, another historian, saw it purely as an economic revolution.24

Dr. Grounds mentioned Richard Shaull who, in the 1970s, was a professor of Ecumenics at Princeton Theological Seminary, in New Jersey. Shaull is quoted as saying that "revolution is to be our [American] destiny."25 This statement is not surprising because any ardent student of American history would have realized that the United States has already gone through three revolutions.

There was the hostile and violent break with Britain in the 1770s – the first revolution. Then, there was the Civil War of 1860 to 1865 –

the second American revolution. There was the era of the Civil Rights Movement – the third American revolution. I believe the U.S. is now at the threshold of its fourth revolution, especially with the upheavals precipitated by the Iraqi and Afghan wars under President George Bush.

An interesting aspect of our search for the meaning of the term revolution is Vernon Grounds's notion of what he calls "the phenomenon of total revolution," an idea which he shares with such authors like Richard Shaull, John A. T. Robinson of the <u>Honest to God</u> fame, Richard John Neuhaus and John McHale, author of the book, <u>The Future of the Future</u> (1968).

In particular is Grounds's reference to Neuhaus, who wrote as follows:

> We are for revolution. A revolution of consciousness, no doubt. A cultural revolution, certainly. A non-violent revolution, perhaps. An armed overthrow of the existing order, it may be necessary. Revolution for the hell of it or revolution for a new world, but revolution, yes.26

But Grounds cautioned against our being the prototype of Rip Van Winkle of Sleepy Hollow fame, or King George III of England, both of whom were the victims of "a somnolent complacency," sleeping while a revolution was going on in the New World.27 We should, rather, be "insurrectionists in the name of God."28

We should not think that Grounds meant that one should become a radical, fundamentalist, Islamic Jihadist, ready to blow up innocent children at school or patients in a hospital, all for the sake of a revolution. I believe that what Grounds meant was that our lives must be revolutionary as to affect change, fundamental change for good in another person's life. This is the transformation of "the human environment and of man himself. …"29

We ought to understand that the sciences, technologies, economies, religion and political institutions may change. But if there is no transformation of the human soul and spirit, our civilization will remain the same or even worse, with all its perils, faults, omissions and commissions of cruelty and barbarisms. This is the kind of revolutionary change which I want for my motherland – Africa.

As I have stated elsewhere, I am not a hard-nosed capitalist, communist, socialist or welfarist.30 I am for beauty within the spirit, decency, fairness, love and the treatment of our fellow human being as our brother or sister. We may have all the money that we want to and build all the skyscrapers that we can. But without some virtues and values, we labor in vain and Africa will continue to be plagued by her many vicissitudes.

Grounds pointed to Karl Marx's statement that a revolution is "the locomotive of all history."31 Virtues, as the history of man has shown, comprise the fuel for the locomotive of history. My motto for an African revolution is: peace, love and freedom. When Thomas Kanza wrote in 1978 that Africa must change, he called his work "an African Manifesto."32

Africans need to understand what kind of revolution is necessary for their sustainable development in the future. Africans must change for the sake of peace, love and freedom. Africa cannot forever be lost in the abyss of blind or crude traditionalism – good or bad. In this exercise toward a definition for revolution, I urge Africans to embrace a revolutionary change that is vital and meaningful for human survival.

The African world revolution, as historian John Henrik Clarke called it,33 must be what Grounds termed a total revolution which embraced all of the areas of the African life: marriage and family, culture, religion, education, economics, militarism, nationhood, ethnicity, race, and foreign or international relations and trade. African revolution must include our view of the African man and woman and their views of or responses to exploitation, prosperity, materialism and their destinies.

In one of my earliest publications, I had argued that Africans cannot and should not continue to be the world's perpetual survivalists.34 We ought to grow and move fast beyond that level to become actualists – a race of people who have arrived, like the Jews, and are making it at the center of the global village.

We Africans ought to discover the relevant and proper meaning of the term, revolution, not that which will bring to us racial suicide but definitely that which will take us to a new place beyond the Afro-pessimism of the present.35

This is what I yearn for myself and for my two wonderful children, and my grandchildren. I believe that the Barack Obama revolution has brought into focus our present and future perspectives regarding the meaning of an African revolution. What is left is how we must sustain this kind of revolution without bloodshed.

In the chapter that follows, I will attempt to examine the origin of a different kind of revolution, namely, the <u>celestial revolution</u>, which is my justification for daring to talk about an African revolution.

CHAPTER TWO
The Origin Of Revolution

Before the dawn of what we now know as human history, there was a revolution – a celestial revolution — the first ever recorded story of a revolution with great cosmic consequences and significance. Here is a succinct and brief account of it in the Bible (Revelation 12: 7-9):

> And there was war in heaven. Michael and his angels fought against the dragon, and the dragon and his angels fought back. But he was not strong enough, and they lost their place in heaven. The great dragon was hurled down – that ancient serpent called the devil or Satan, who leads the whole world astray. He was hurled to the earth, and his angels with him.

In this very short but precise and descriptive narrative, we find the ingredients for a revolution. First, there was a clash of interests (Isaiah 14: 12-17), with no one party willing to compromise or yield to the opposition. Then, there was a clash of authority or power. The two contending powers or authorities could not co-exist. Either one wanted to remain in complete power and, as the text above indicates, the devil sought to usurp heavenly power . The result was war.

Second, there was a threat to the status quo. In the infinite wisdom of God Almighty, the devil or Satan was embattled and defeated. God triumphed over Satan. This defeat of Satan led to his expulsion from the celestial realm. Satan and his forces, comprising about a third of the angelic beings that existed at the time, were forced to retreat to planet earth. They have been here ever since that expulsion. Thus, a fundamental change had occurred.

Third, we may never know with certainty why God and this archangel, Michael did not completely annihilate Satan and his evil forces but allowed them to retreat to our planet. What is obvious is that there was war in heaven where God is supposed to reign as sovereign. God's forces overthrew the rebels. That war created an opportunity for Satan to transact his diabolical plans and schemes against God and man.

It may be difficult for the average man to conceive of a rebellion or a revolution in heaven. But the Bible says so. Today, more than a billion professing Christians believe the Bible. In another Bible passage, the motive for that ancient rebellion is provided. Satan's motives for rebellion did not emerge from some pure and virtuous impulses (see Ezekiel 28: 12-19).

Rather, Satan's motives came out of vices such as pride, arrogance, envy, jealousy, selfishness and intolerance. In a word, Satan's motives came from sin. Ezekiel 28: 15 reads: "You were blameless in your ways from the day you were created till wickedness was found in you." Verse 17 of this chapter reads: "Your heart became proud on account of your beauty, and you corrupted your wisdom because of your splendor." There, we have it.

Satan was definitely a created being like many of us. He was a highly exalted being until his ambitions corrupted him. Verses 12 to 17 of Isaiah 14 tell us more:

> How have you fallen from heaven, O morning star, son of the dawn! You have been cast down to the earth, you who once laid low the nations! You said in your heart, 'I will ascend to heaven, I will raise my throne above the stars of God; I will sit enthroned on the mount of the assembly, on the utmost heights of the sacred mountain. I will ascend above the tops of the clouds; I will make myself like the Most High.'"

We ought to note at once the five self-and ill-motivated impulses for rebellion against God's authority and power. The fifth reason for Satan's act of usurpation is quite revealing – he envied the high position that God occupied in His celestial kingdom. Satan despised the principal office which he held at the time among the angels. He wanted God's position. He wanted to be God Almighty!

The celestial revolution came out of some inward, demonic impulses which were vicious and wicked. Satan's diabolical plan was nursed within himself but executed in the deceitful mobilization of a third of the angelic hosts who conspired against God. When they lost the battle, they became rebels without divine sanction.

These angelic rebels had underestimated God's infinite omnipotence, omniscience, omnipresence and sovereign will. They lost His love for them. The result was their expulsion from their celestial realm (Ezekiel 28: 16) and cast out into the abyss of earthly darkness where Satan has become the prince of darkness. He is still so.

In the book of Jude in the Bible, we have a seemingly concluding statement about this abortive revolution which I have been analyzing: "And the angels who did not keep their positions of authority but abandoned their home ... these he has kept in darkness bound with everlasting chains for judgment on the great Day" (verse 6). We are then warned to recognize legitimate power and authority (verses 8-10).

Even though defeated, Satan's powers and authority seem to be recognized by Michael in 2 Peter 2: 10-12. A military General is always a military General until he or she is stripped of his or her title and rank. However, our recognition of Satan's authority and power does not necessarily imply acquiescence with his wicked, arbitrary or totalitarian power or authority.

Believers in Christ Jesus are commanded to "resist the devil and he will flee from us" (I Peter 5: 6). In this sense, Satan is supposed to be under our feet. Also, we can deduce from all this analysis that when people think of revolution, they often think of a military conflict involving political, social, and economic conflicts and their consequences.

But the celestial revolution seems to me to have been a religious or even a spiritual conflict, don't you think so? We should never forget that this conflict first began in heaven. So, we can formulate a theology for revolution from this encounter.

We must clearly understand the biblical passages quoted in this analysis and their implications for other revolutionary causes or action. The first implication is that not all revolutions are bad and not all revolutions are good, either. The motivations for any revolution is of paramount importance. Motivation relates to the success or failure of the revolution.

We should note that God did not arbitrarily hinder the revolution but allowed it to commence and proceed. But He did not condone nor tolerate it beyond a point. For, had the Satanic revolution succeeded, we would have had serious implications for our theology about God and His universe. It is shocking even to think of what would have happened to our Almighty God.

What would have happened to mankind had Satan become our everlasting God? Have you ever given any serious thought about this question? What, if the unseen and spiritual world was dominated and ruled absolutely by vices and evil spirits without the counterbalancing redemptive power of a Holy God at work?

The second implication we should consider from the heavenly revolution is that anyone who contemplates a revolution must consider his or her motivations, intentions and purposes for the revolution. Some very serious questions must be asked, such as: "is the revolution ill-motivated, diabolical and selfish? Is the revolution based upon greed, envy, and covetousness?

Suppose that the revolution fails, then what?" There must be some guiding principles for the revolution. The planners of earthly revolutions are blessed by the fact that human beings are not omniscient nor omnipresent. Or, they would be in serious trouble right from the beginning. But any revolutionary leader must remember that the price for failure is often death.

A revolutionary leader must always remember the words credited to Chairman Mao when he said that "A revolution is not a dinner party."2 He or she must consider what spiritual forces are behind the intended action. For a Christian revolutionary, he should remember the biblical statement that the instruments of our warfare are not carnal but spiritual and mighty THROUGH GOD to demolish evil opposition (2 Cor. 10:4).

The third implication we should consider is that some revolutions are, at times, irrepressible or inevitable. For instance, historians are still asking whether the American Civil War was an irrepressible conflict or not? But, was the Second World War inevitable? I think that the war was inevitable since Hitler's evil designs had to be eliminated.

Since Hitler turned fellow whites into powder and soap, what do we black people think he would have done to the people of African descent? If I can play the apologist for God, let me ask: "what was God supposed to do in the face of Satan's diabolical plans? Was God supposed to accommodate Satan's evil and wild ambitions?" God forbid!

Was God supposed to negotiate some terms of amity with Satan and his rebel forces? Was God supposed to turn the other cheek, as some conscientious objectors to war might want us to? We do not have all the answers to these questions because we are not God.

But, what we do know is very clear: there was a rebellion in heaven. It was a doomed revolution. God crushed the rebellion and maintained law and order. Satan was forced to retreat, and unfortunately, he arrived at planet Earth. We now have to contend with him. Life involves a definite spiritual warfare and nobody can avoid it.

With respect to Satan's evil plot against the human race, God had lovingly predestinated His own designs for mankind's redemption through the atoning work of Jesus Christ upon the Cross. The amazing thing is that many people are fully aware of this loving act of God and they refuse to accept it. How sad.

Often, I suspect that Satan had no idea of the secret plan of God. Remember that Satan is not omniscient. He did not figure out the great depth of God's marvelous LOVE for man (John 3:16). Satan did not understand that God's mercies, grace, and compassion for man are inestimable.

Had Satan any foreknowledge of the great mind of God, maybe, he would not have embarked upon such a suicidal plot. And, unfortunately, most people on this earth have no idea how much God loves them. They have never discovered how excellent God is. They have foolishly bought the ancient lie of Satan, namely, that God is a bad God who is undeserving of complete worship, praise and adoration. Those who love God need not rebel against Him.

Being themselves dominated by greed, envy, jealousy, covetousness and sin (just like Satan), it is no wonder that the same Satanic impulses despise God and they strive to destroy all that is good in God's wonderful and beautiful creation. They do not seem to realize that they are doing the job of the old liar and serpent, the devil.

But, salvation simply consists in being on God's side of the human drama and committing oneself to God's program for planet Earth. To be on the other side is to be a rebel in God's kingdom. Oh, how much God loves men and women.

The theological ramifications of any revolutionary cause or action imply that we must recognize evil, all kinds of evil, for what it is and determine to eschew and destroy it, by God's help. Here, there is no room for neutrality. We must possess a revolutionary mind regarding the activities of Satan, the arch-rebel, evil and all the other forces of evil. We must be radical about such a perspective.3 This is what Africa needs, now.

A theology for revolution implies that we accept responsibility for the destruction of evil. We cannot be apathetic about this. It is only in this sense that we can fully appreciate the meaning of Edmund Burke's words when he once said that "the only thing necessary for the triumph of evil is for good men to do nothing."4 These are the kind of revolutionaries who will save Africa. They will include the insurrectionists for Christ.

My next chapter examines the necessity for an African revolution. Read on.

CHAPTER THREE
The Necessity For An African Revolution

The average woman in West Africa today is dead before forty after about nine pregnancies. She has a life that any observer would have to classify as miserable. She is not living longer than her mother; the average woman of West Africa of twenty or twenty-five years ago was dead at thirty-six. The same was true at the beginning of the century.1

— Dr. Vernon C. Grounds, 1971.

The African is not an alien to the concept of revolution. As a part of the human race, he is prone to all the vicissitudes which have plagued human society from time immemorial. Someone may think that the term, revolution, only conjures images of khaki-wearing, gun-totting, trigger-happy soldiers who would kill at random during any coup-de-tat or after a putsch.

But, as we saw in Chapter One, a revolution is about a fundamental change to the basic fabric of society. African people, like the Jewish people, know much about human sufferings, oppression, exploitation, and all of man's inhumanity to man, perhaps, much more so than any other human group on the face of the Earth.

Instinctively, the African knows that, in order for him to better his condition of life, there must constantly be change – significant and fundamental change or changes toward that betterment of life. I would say, with some degree of accuracy, that the African has engaged in some revolutionary movements and changes that have already shaped or reshaped most parts of the world, including his own. Just think of the Haitian Revolution of 1803!

Just as the central theme of African American history is freedom, the central theme of postcolonial African life and history has been the quest for complete freedom or liberty from foreign domination. Truly, Africans as a whole have not yet arrived. For many of them, it is not yet <u>uhuru</u>.2 Hence the necessity for a total revolution.

During the early years of the struggle for decolonization, Frantz Fanon, born in 1925 in the Caribbean island of Martinique, emerged as one of the spokesmen for authentic African revolution. In 1961, the year that he died at the age of 36, Fanon published <u>The Wretched of the Earth</u>, his most internationally popular book, which has now been translated into 25 languages, with over a million copies in the English language alone.3

Vernon C. Grounds, already cited, quotes Fanon as saying that the "radical transformation of society" is imperative even if it entails "being caught up in a veritable Apocalyse."4 Drawing his insights from the Algerian War for Independence from the French, Fanon offered a "brilliant examination of the role of violence in effecting historical change."5

Fanon's powerful collection of articles, essays and letters were posthumously published in 1964 under the title, <u>Toward the African Revolution</u>, which signified that Fanon was deeply concerned with the necessity for an African revolution. In this book, Fanon argued that "colonialism is fundamentally inexcusable."6

Fanon also stated that "it is a liberated individual who undertakes to build the new society."7 The building of such a new society, a postcolonial society, entailed a revolutionary change from the experiences of the past. In <u>The Wretched of the Earth</u>, Fanon pleaded: "For Europe, for ourselves, and for humanity, comrades, we must turn over a new leaf; we must work out new concepts, and try to set about a new man."8

It is clear here that Fanon was concerned with revolutionary concepts that would produce a new man, not just new institutions. Although Africa was having so many coups (73 of them by 1985, according to one observer),9 the continent, in my judgment, had not yet given birth to an authentic revolution, whether in the social, political, economic, intellectual or religious realm.

Currently, there appears to be no new leaders emerging out of Africa, to enthrone the kind of revolutionary changes which Fanon conceived of. Instead, as author Barry Rubin has eloquently argued in his book, <u>Modern Dictators: Third World Coup Makers, Strongmen, and Populist Tyrants</u> (1987), Africa is run by people with no visionary ideas and kleptocrats who have betrayed the African dream and brought immense chaos to the Africans. Nelson Mandela is today the only exception.

Given the above situation, the African American historian John Henrik Clarke, rightly queried: "Who betrayed the African world revolution?"10 His question implied that there was an African world revolution in progress. Clarke said that from Trinidad came a Pan-Africanist conception of the world and it was a lawyer, Henry Sylvester, who first coined the term, Pan-Africanism.11

Clarke maintained that it was C. L. R. James and George Padmore, both from Trinidad, along with W. E. B. Du Bois who "gave the concept of Pan-Africanism form and substance."12 He argued that Pan-Africanism envisaged the unity of all peoples of African descent in all the continents of the world. But, it was the lack of such racial unity which gave the Europeans the opportunity to rule and dominate the African race.

So, who and how was the African world revolution betrayed? According to Clarke, first, the contemporary African leaders, the "house-servants" in Africa, colluded with the European powers to thwart the revolution. Next were the Caribbean people who made little use of the Pan-African concept. Then, in addition, were the African American elites, the "confused ideologist, middle-class fakers and just plain sellouts."13

Also, Clarke believed that the American Civil Rights Movement leaders "could have used that moment to call attention to the needs of the African people all over the world, not only [to] call for Pan-Africanism but [for] an African world community."14

Collaborating with the French, British, and America, the concept and the African world community were destroyed. Hence, the African world revolution was destroyed, just as Kwame Nkrumah and his idea of African unity were destroyed.15

It is important to note here that Professor Clarke seemed to have ignored the great ideas and efforts of the Ethiopianists, people like Paul Hall (1748-1807), Paul Cuffe (1759-1817), Robert A. Young (no date of birth), David Walker (1785-1830), Martin Delany (1812-1885), Henry Highland Garnet (1815-1882), Alexander Crummell (1819-1898), Edward Wilmot Blyden (1832-1912), Bishop Henry Turner (1834-1915) and Marcus Garvey (1887-1940).

The above ten men kept the African dream and hope alive, ardently looking forward to the day when Africa, then known as Ethiopia, "shall stretch forth her hands unto God" (Psalm 68:31). They believed that on that day, Africa would receive her blessings and become a continent of greatness and fame.

The Ethiopianists were keepers of the Pan-African dream.16 Their prophetic utterances came to be fulfilled, at least in part, when some African countries regained their independence from European domination around 1960.

As for me, the most criminal betrayers of the African world revolution are the present-day African leaders themselves who, without a proper knowledge of their history and vision, without a mission, have compromised the dreams of many Africans for the sake of greed and selfishness. These so-called leaders have forced many Africans into self-imposed exile and into the diaspora. Their corrupt and wicked style of governance loudly calls for a total revolution. Africans want a revolution now.

Sometimes, the causes that lead to wars are the same ones that may lead to a revolution. Sometimes, they may not. But, we can be sure of this fact: continuous and unbearable human sufferings and miseries will precipitate a revolution. The verdict of history is clear on this point. God has not created human beings with an insatiable appetite for sufferings and miseries in perpetuity!

Among many other reasons, I do believe that the lack of human freedoms and justice; the prevalence of intolerance; crude forms of evil and vices; poverty and hunger; inequality and long-lasting grudges in Africa will necessitate a revolution. Let's examine these seven factors in some detail:

1. LACK OF TRUE FREEDOMS

God did not create human beings to be slaves; otherwise, He simply could have made us to be robots. But some men and women, black and white, have found it convenient and to their benefit to enslave other human beings. They feel entitled or justified to do so.

Wherever slavery exists, whether in ancient Egypt or in America, there the seeds for a revolution are sown. Only time can tell when the revolution would be born. This is the hard lesson that many slave-masters have refused to learn.

And so, in spite of the end of historical slavery, the modern Sudanese and Mauritanian governments in Africa still practice slavery.17 There are many people held in slavery in the Middle Eastern countries where Africans had been sold into slavery.

Dr. Billy Graham wrote about such a case of slavery which existed about 1212 A.D. Thousands of European youths, mostly French and German, were deceived and carried away into slavery when their ships first docked in Algeria and in Egypt. Those youths were "dispersed all over the Saracen empire; the children were never heard from again."18

In today's Darfur region in the Sudan, the slavery there has been well documented in spite of the denials of the Sudanese government.19 The hope of these unfortunate slaves is that a revolution will be launched someday that will liberate them from their bondage. Sadly, it is the Arab Africans who are oppressing the dark-skinned Africans!

In many parts of Africa and the modern world, there are serious efforts to check the trafficking in children. The Federal Government of Nigeria has a task force on this matter. Many Nigerian children are deceived and sold into European prostitution markets and they are often seen on the streets of Italy and other European capital cities! Who says that we don't need a revolution?

God will surely send a Moses, a deliverer, to those enslaved no matter how long their captivity have been. God is a God of freedom and liberty. Tyranny, despotism, dictatorships and certain kinds of human rights abuses also breed serfdom and lack of freedom. Africans have had their fair share of mistreatment from cruel colonial masters, and, now, from their own home-bred so-called leaders! The former ruler of Uganda, Idi Amin, typifies this college of modern-day despots and dictators.

But, centuries ago, Thomas Jefferson, one of the founding fathers of the American Republic, wrote that man is endowed by his Creator with certain inalienable rights, and that among these were life, liberty, and the pursuit of happiness. Another American philosopher, Dr. Elton Trueblood, elaborated on the Jeffersonian principles when he stated that there were truly only six positive freedoms, namely, the freedom to learn, debate, worship, serve, live and work.20

Some other forms of freedoms include the right to equality and the dignity of the life of the individual. The first here protects one from discrimination, segregation, sexism, racial and religious abuses. The second protects one from bodily harm resulting from rapes and torture. Currently, agism is a matter of public concern where one can be denied a job simply because of one's age.

In many parts of Africa today, the state is a god, a titanic and unassailable entity that can preserve, protect or take away any human life. Power is retained by the state rather than by the people who are seen as slaves of the system. The individual is reduced to a number or statistic. The people are systematically disenfranchised by intimidation or state-sponsored terrorism.

Is there any wonder , then, that a revolution is on the way? I remind all who read these lines that Menachem Begin, the former Israeli Prime Minister, once stated that "if you love freedom, you must hate slavery."21 That is the maxim by which all Africans should live and die. Africans need to reiterate the famous statement Patrick Henry made while fighting for freedom for the American colonies. He declared: "Give me Liberty, or Give Me Death."

2. INJUSTICES

It is very painful for me to write about some injustices which many Africans have been subjected to by their own very people. Currently, the media has reported on these injustices such as cases of politically-motivated assassinations, murders and the dismemberment of the bodies of the victims in order to conceal the evidence.

There are social, political, religious and economic injustices perpetrated all the time. In Nigeria, for example, the Niger Delta crisis is about whole scale environmental injustice. It is also related to economic injustice. Cruelty to prisoners and their imprisonment are some of the modern heinous crimes and barbarism meted out to fellow Africans. Life is very cheap! For a few dollars, one could be hired to commit murder without any arrest of the criminal.

Generally speaking, there is no respect for <u>due process</u>. Many of these injustices are simply violations of the human rights and civil liberties of fellow Africans. The Nigeria Police is very corrupt, inefficient, and sometimes, unable or unwilling to deal with criminal incidents. They collect bribes publicly on the roads. There is no secret about it.

It is not only the Police Force that is corrupt. The whole social, religious and political system is very corrupt. One has to bribe his or her way through in order to live there. In Nigeria, the popular saying is: "If you cannot beat the system, join it." And so, many of the young graduates, without jobs, have joined the system.

Someone may ask me: "How do I know these things?" I am a Nigerian intellectual elite and I read the papers and listen to the news media. I am also a keen observer of the society. Besides, I am a well-trained historian who is more than an average reader. I am supposed to know what happens in my world.

Believe me when I say that the ordinary Nigerian is longing for a revolution. On April 4, 2008, Sulaimon Olanrewaju, a journalist and reporter with the <u>Nigerian Tribune</u> newspaper, was cited to have covered a book launch in which some prominent Nigerians called for a revolution for Nigeria.

Four of the seven Nigerians cited called for a bloody revolution. Their names were given as Professor Ben Nwabueze, an acclaimed constitutional law scholar, Chief Orji Kalu, former governor of Abia state, Chief Olisa Agbakoba, of the Nigerian Bar Association, and Bola Tinubu, the former governor of Lagos state.

Those who called for a peaceful revolution in Nigeria were Babatunde Fashola, the current governor of Lagos state, Lieutenant General Theophilus Danjuma, and Chief G. O. K. Ajayi. Since that date, many more Nigerians have joined in the call for a revolution in Nigeria. As Nigeria goes, so goes Africa. The call for revolution is in response to the widening gap between the haves and the have-nots in Nigeria.

The revolution is bound to come because exploitation, oppression, evil governance and insecurity cannot last forever. I repeat that God is a God of freedom, justice and righteousness. He will never, never acquit the evil-doer and the ungodly.

3. INTOLERANCE

Because I have discussed this matter in an earlier book, <u>LISTEN AFRICANS: Freedom is Under Fire</u> (2002), I will only update the material here. Intolerance occurs more and more in Africa today in the realm of religion. The combatants are often Muslims and Christians.

In a country like Nigeria, Muslims have been killing Christians at random in the northern part, partly due to inadequate police protection. As a result, Christians have started to retaliate. In 2007, some high school students of a Government Secondary School located at Gandu in Gombe State, publicly murdered their female teacher named Mrs Oluwatoyin C. Oluwaseesin, mother of two little children, for "desecrating" the Koran.

The students had allegedly gone into an examination hall with materials intending to cheat. When their teacher found out, she threw out the materials from the classroom. Premeditatedly, those students later attacked their teacher and beat her to death.22 The public was told she had "desecrated" the Koran.

These criminals were NOT even arrested at the time that the story was reported. This is usually the case when a Christian is the victim. Why would anybody in Nigeria, <u>who is not a Muslim</u>, want to be the constant victim of those who are bent upon the Islamization of the entire country of Nigeria through cruelty such as the case of Mrs. Oluwaseesin? Why would a Christian want to be part of such a country? Thus, a revolution is coming and it is inevitable! Let the Muslims continue to Darfurianize Nigeria.

It does not matter whether Nigeria has one million soldiers or ten million soldiers under orders to keep Nigeria one. One day, the soldiers whose relatives are constantly the victims of Islamic cruelties, will mutiny and revolt. Where were the soldiers when Islamic Nigerians slaughtered Christians recently in Jos and Bauchi in northern Nigeria?

Thomas Paine, author of the book, <u>Common Sense</u>, once wrote that "toleration is not the opposite of intolerance, but is the counterfeit of it."23 The victims of religious intolerance are not asking for the guarantees of religious toleration in their God-given native land. They

21

are demanding for religious FREEDOM which has already been allowed under the <u>United Nations Declaration of Human Rights of 1948</u>, a document to which almost all the African countries are signatories. Without religious freedom, a revolution is inevitable in Africa. It ought to be obvious to anyone that religious wars are very hard to deal with. If Biafra was able to hold Nigeria to a 30-month civil war, what makes anyone in Northern Nigeria to think that a religious war would be settled in a matter of weeks? One ought to remember what happened in northern Ireland between the Catholics and Protestants.

Nor should one forget the recent crisis between Shiites and Sunnis in Iraq. Nobody should take the patience of Nigerian Christians for granted. Even this writer would be very willing to give up his life in the event of such a war. The patience of the Christians is almost running out!

Whether the Islamic imperialism or threat to common freedoms in Africa is real or a myth will depend upon the degree of the "freedom of religion" which the African Christians are able to enjoy.24 Anything less will necessitate a revolution. My belief is that a revolution is just around the corner and time will tell. Listen Africans, a religious revolution is coming. And, come it must!

4. GROWING ACTS OF WICKEDNESS

The vices and evil which we know as greed, envy, jealousy and covetousness can lead to glaring and growing acts of wickedness. Where these abound, a revolution is inescapable. The regime or government which condones or tolerates gross acts of wickedness by man against his or her fellow man cannot long exist.

It ought to be clear to the African policy-makers that evil and wickedness are counterproductive to the well-being of the state. This is why good laws are made. Those who violate the good laws of a nation ought to be punished so as to keep intending offenders away from their crimes. Vices and wickedness never do anyone any good.

Any leader who thinks he or she can prosper or benefit from growing acts of wickedness is deceiving himself or herself. Simply stated, revolutions occur because people are dissatisfied within the political realm. Discontentment is never a boon to any successful regime.

Therefore, it would be wise to avoid national conditions which breed discontentment. When the French people grew discontented in 1789, they blew up the Establishment. The African governments must eschew growing acts of wickedness and the governance which is based upon evil devices. This is one way to avoid a bloody revolution.

In the Bible, King Ahab had grown greedy, brutal and bloody. His wife was not called Jezebel for being a mother Teresa. No one, including the Ahab clan, thought their regime would come to an end. Ahab had 70 sons, not counting his daughters. Then, one day, it happened. Ahab was killed in a military conflict. The young revolutionary, Jehu, subsequently appeared at the doorsteps of the palace and threw Jezebel out to the dogs who ate her up. All the 70 sons of Ahab were killed in one day. The game was over for the Ahab family (I King.22:34-38 and 2 King.9: 35-37). I hope that someone is listening!

5. POVERTY AND HUNGER

At the beginning of this Chapter, I quoted a statement made by Dr. Vernon C. Grounds regarding the poverty and living conditions of the average West African woman. That statement was made in 1971, some 38 years ago. Though, perhaps, the statement may be a bit exaggerated, the conditions of life which Grounds wrote of, in all honesty, have today deteriorated, with increasing wars and corruption. While the rest of the world is marching forward, Africa is retrogressing.

Thirty years ago, when I first arrived in the United States, one Nigerian naira was worth nearly two dollars. Thereafter, we had currency devaluations upon devaluations in keeping with the World Bank and the International Monetary Fund (IMF) wonderful advices. Today, one naira is worth 1/150 of a dollar, that is, one needs 150 naira to exchange for a dollar!

This goes to show the truth behind what Grounds wrote of. The Africans are caught in the grip of international schemes and conditions which have rendered their currencies worthless and, thus, their purchasing power is limited. All this is happening in spite of the wealth and riches of the continent.

The above situation also means that the living conditions of the average African has deteriorated. Africans have gotten poorer and poorer while hunger persists. This condition is unacceptable because we Africans know that we could have done better. Our hunger and poverty are recipes for revolution. As we say in Africa, "a hungry man is an angry man."

Poverty and economic injustices are related. A prosperous and caring country is one that tends to alleviate hunger and starvation. Economic justice and good governance take care of the poor and the hungry.25 When people are well-fed and satisfied, they tend to avoid armed- belligerence and violence because they begin to think of other creative ways of living, such as inventions in the arts and sciences.

The popular saying is that necessity is the mother of inventions but it did not say that poverty or starvation breeds creativity. The only reason why the hungry masses have not gone wild and violent is that they fear for their lives because they know that their governments can be very brutal and destroy them. They have no love for the state; they have fear for it! Think about this for a moment.

Those who rule Africa today must be sure of this: God is a God of the poor and the oppressed. There is a special place in His heart for them.26 The poor and hungry in Africa will not wait until they become cannibals. This is one reason why the region of Darfur in the Sudan had exploded. The Khartoum government will not forever be able to hold down the hungry ones in Darfur through armed aggression.

Somewhere, I read a statement credited to Nelson Mandela who said that as long as there is poverty and hunger anywhere, there is no freedom. I agree. Since there is enough food available in this world to feed everyone, it is deliberate genocide to allow anyone to starve to death. It ought to be criminal and punishable by imprisonment to use food and starvation as instruments of state-sponsored terrorism or war.

6. THE MENACE OF INEQUALITY

Truly, no country can thrive or survive for long under conditions of human inequality. The United States did not. She was an independent Republic for 84 years (1776-1860), but practicing different kinds of inequalities against a segment of her population – against the African Americans who were held in slavery.

Then, there exploded a fireball in the night which engulfed the entire country for about five years (1860-1865). This was the terrible

American Civil War or, as some scholars have called it, the Second American Revolution. But, in reality, this revolution did not end the age-old practices of inequalities through discrimination, segregation, and the practices of Jim Crow, even though actual chattel slavery came to an end.

A third American Revolution had to come because there is something in man that will always resist oppression and injustices. The Civil Rights Movement which began in the 1960s was necessitated by the need to address the unfinished work of the second revolution. Thus, we hear of "40 acres and a mule" which many African Americans are yet still to receive.

Equality, the opposite of inequality, is rooted in the belief that all men and women, even children, are created equal. Thus, <u>equality is a moral imperative for freedom</u>. Those who love freedom and yet despise equality are fools. Freedom cannot be sustained in a culture of inequalities. Thomas Paine, one of the pillars in the American Revolution, said: "I believe in one God and no more ... I believe in the equality of man."27

Robert Maynard Hutchins (1899-1977), another great American, stated that "equality and justice, the two great distinguishing characteristics of democracy, follow inevitably from the conception of men, all men, as rational and spiritual beings."28 Also, Thomas Jefferson summed it up when he wrote: "We hold these truths to be self-evident; that all men are created equal."29

Therefore, any country governed by just laws demands that there be equality included in the law for all men, women and children. In their common humanity, the philosopher Mortimer J. Adler contended, all human beings are equal. However, in Africa, inequality is like racism which, by definition, assumes the superiority of one person over and above another. Thus, a racist can discriminate against another human being based solely upon prejudice and a supposed inferiority status.

Actions that result from this stance of inequality are a sin and a violation of the rights of one's humanity. For a long time in South Africa, apartheid based on the superiority of white people was a national sin. In many instances, inequality becomes a tool used for the mistreatment, exploitation and oppression of some people. It can be a discriminatory tool used to exclude others from enjoying certain rights.

Africans should understand that a person thus mistreated suffers a significant amount of pain. The caste system in some African societies is a case in point. The mistreated person does suffer from some kinds of emotional, mental and physical pain that may become traumatic. Tribalism can also be a tool for inequality.

Called ethnicity by some scholars, tribalism is the African equivalence of racism. In the former instance, a person is mistreated solely because of race or skin color. In the latter case, one is mistreated solely due to membership in a separate or different ethnic group. The place of one's birth may determine who belongs to or does not belong to the particular ethnic group.

Thus, one may be an Akan, Ashanti, Igbo, Yoruba, Hausa, Mandingo, Ibibio or Fulani. In my judgment, tribalism was at the root of the 1994 massacres in Rwanda. There may have been some religious, political and economic reasons. But I believe that tribalism was at the very core of the conflict. Since the one who suffers from tribalism knows that he or she is being mistreated, they will either tolerate the mistreatment as long as they can, or resist it.

This act of resistance, when properly organized and heightened, may eventually lead to a protest, a rebellion, or a revolution. Since there are many cases of mistreatments in Africa that are due to tribalism, one should not be naïve as to think that a social revolution, meant to ameliorate these vices, is not possible in Africa in the near future.

Inequality is a cankerworm that eats into the very fabric of a society. Therefore, let me say unequivocally that no ordinary African is asking the rulers for the political, social, economic, religious, and intellectual freedoms and equalities in the absolute sense. All that the ordinary African is asking for is simply the equality of humanity, for the liberty which justice allows. He demands no more and no less.

Africans do not want to live perpetually in George Orwell's Animal Farm community. Any African tyrant or despot who thinks otherwise will soon discover that a revolution is standing by the corner. God made us all equal and no man, not even Machiavelli, can justify a negation of His decrees.

7. LONG-STANDING GRUDGES

What is a grudge? The dictionary defines a grudge as "a feeling of deep-seated resentment or ill-will ... malice."30 Malice is defined as ill-will, the "intent to commit an unlawful act or cause harm without legal justification or excuse." Additionally, "malice may imply a deep-seated and often unreasonable dislike and a desire to see one suffer or it may suggest a causeless passing mischievous impulse."31

Seung-Hui Cho (1984-2007) was a Virginia Tech college student from Korea who murdered 32 people and wounded 25 others in April 2007 because he had a grudge against rich people. There may or may not be just causes for a grudge. The primary ingredient is that there is a deep-seated resentment against a person, persons or a whole community.

The public expression of a grudge is a fracas or brawl. Here are some examples. I believe that most people who belong to the Ku Klux Klan (KKK) have grudges against blacks and other racial groups. In 2007 in the Eti-osa Local Government area of Lagos State in Nigeria, "an unidentified 8-year-old pupil rushing to school ... was cut down by hot lead of the bullet(s) by one of the warring factions"32 in the community crisis involving land disputes.

The hostilities occurred in the town of Ajah. Five other people were allegedly matcheted to death as their market stalls were burned down. This mayhem took place in March 2007; but Ajah had suffered a similar fate in 2006. The cause of these incidents were due to land disputes between two families: the Olumegbon and the Ojupons. Obviously, there was a long-standing grudge between the two families.

Land disputes are rampant causes of conflict all over Africa. Anayo Okoli, a journalist reporting from the town of Abakiliki in Eastern Nigeria, stated that 12 people were murdered and 73 houses were destroyed in the Osile/Ogbunike crisis.

The cause of this crisis was alleged to be a plot to dethrone John Umenyiora, the traditional ruler of the town of Ogbunike. Okoli added that the fight was "a war between brothers and sisters"33 who, at times, bore the same names. Quite likely, there was a grudge between them.

Another journalist by the name of Christopher Isiguzo reported that 15 people were murdered and 50 arrested following the "lingering communal crisis in Onicha and Igboeze communities in the Onicha Local Government area of Ebonyi State."34 The fighting there began on

February 2, 2007. Properties belonging to some high profile politicians, including that of the State Deputy Governor, were destroyed.

Over in East Africa, in the Turkana District of northern Kenya, near Lake Turkana which borders the Sudan, "cattle raids are not too uncommon in [the] society."35 Hence the reporter, Ikeny Kapua wrote that "we have become weary of raids."36 Since the life of the local people depends on livestock, such raids can lead to war which, in turn, may sow the seeds for an economic revolution in the area.

The mere suspicion of a person or a family as being a witch can lead to serious community violence and deaths. It is very common in Africa to attribute many predicaments to witchcraft. One woman allegedly blamed her husband for not passing her examinations in the United States because her husband's family had witches who hindered her success. And, a witch is never tolerated nor offered the benefit of a doubt, let alone innocence. Generally, one is guilty if accused!

I believe that rooted in many of these social malaises are long-standing grudges or malice. Africans need to learn the art of conflict resolution, reconciliation and peaceful co-existence. In the three examples of violence which I listed above, which took place in Nigeria in 2007, 33 lives were lost unnecessarily.

There was no forgiveness nor toleration. Bishop Desmond Tutu of South Africa wrote that where there is no forgiveness, there is no future.37 Africans need to heed the wise admonition or counsel by Tutu, otherwise, revolutions based upon mere grudges or malice will continue to plague the continent.

The seven points which I have provided in this chapter as factors which can ultimately cause a revolution ought to be taken seriously by African sociologists and all who love the continent and care for her future prosperity. We Africans should bear in mind the words credited to an anonymous Nigerian complainant who said: "You ... need to know that we Nigerians have a potential for revolution."38

Given what is happening in Nigeria since the general election of 2007 and all over the motherland, Africans are ripe for a revolution. But what kind of revolution will it be? Peaceful or bloody? The choice is for us Africans to make. But we must be sure of this: a revolution is coming!

CHAPTER FOUR
Theological Basis For African Revolution

To the ordinary and unsophisticated mind, the subject for our consideration is both difficult and controversial. But since many Africans are "notoriously religious," according to the eminent scholar and author, John S. Mbiti, and belong to either the Christian or Muslim faith, we must try to present a careful theological basis for an African revolution.

In Chapter One, I had defined what is a revolution. In this chapter, I try to define what is theology. The term theology comes from two Greek words – theos, meaning God and logos, meaning word or a "reasoned discourse."1 Therefore, theology "is the application of principles of logical thought to truth about theos, God."2

"Theology is the exhibition of the facts of Scripture in their proper order and relation with the principles or general truths involved in the facts themselves, and which pervade and harmonize the whole."3 Since there is a Christian theology ("the science of Christianity"4), one may also speak of an Islamic theology.

There are other kinds of theologies: natural, systematic, biblical, historical, applied, and revolutionary. Dr. Vernon C. Grounds, in his book, Revolution and the Christian Faith, devoted an entire chapter to what he called "The Theology of Revolution."5

In another chapter of his book, Grounds also discussed what he called "Jesus the Revolutionary."6 He concluded his work with an analysis of "Revolutionary Christianity."7 Hence, we should not be shocked nor alarmed when I contend that there ought to be a proper understanding of a theology for the African revolution drawing upon the path already laid down by many other experts on this subject.

I am simply putting into context what is available in the writings on our topic (historiography).8 For instance, John Kenneth Galbraith, the renowned Harvard University professor of Economics and author of more than 30 books, once stated that "a man cannot live without an economic theology."9 In like manner, I contend that no man who believes in any kind of radical socio-political change can live without a revolutionary theology.

By revolutionary theology, I mean a concept of the relations between a man, his God, and the processes which lead to radical, fundamental changes in society for the good or betterment of such a society. If such a man is an African, he or she ought to have an African revolutionary theology. An African revolutionary theology, therefore, means the application of such a concept to the African situation. This is called contextualization.

It is important that the Christian or Muslim or any advocate of the traditional African religion understands how his or her faith relates to social, political, and economic change or changes. This is the burden of what is called Church-state studies.

There should be no dichotomy or disconnection between one's faith and the socio-political or even economic as well as the intellectual theology one holds. I believe that such a dichotomy is tantamount to the possession of poor or bad theology,

Pericles (495-429 B.C.), the ancient Athenian philosopher once said: "We believe a man should be concerned about public as well as private affairs, for we regard the person who takes no part in politics not as merely uninterested but as useless."10 Being interested in public affairs means being engaged in political theology.

Some Christians have become so heavenly minded that they are of no earthly use. They have forgotten that they were supposed to be the salt and the light of the world. But, I believe that it is the duty of Africans, particularly in the field of systematic theology, to do the great work of synthesizing faith and politics for our people. We should no longer wait for Europeans to do this for us.

In this regard, I applaud the efforts of Tom Skinner, the late African American evangelical and author of the book, <u>Words of Revolution</u>

(1970). Skinner believed that "if the message of Jesus Christ is to have intellectual integrity and validity for our time, it must speak to the issues."11 Also, I believe that a spiritual current underlies every effective initiative that leads to fundamental changes in society. Therefore, a revolutionary change ought to have a sound theological basis.

Some people may recoil from the idea of revolution because they consider that war and theology (or even their personal faith) have nothing in common. Such people still hold firm to the archaic, traditional or even antiquated view that a revolution always means wars which include killings, bombings, use of weapons of mass destruction, genocide, pogroms, anarchy and chaos. This is the old school of thinking about war.

I would therefore like to refer advocates of the old school ideas on Christianity and war to the conclusions made by authors David L. Clough and Brian Stiltner in their recent book, <u>Faith and Force: A Christian Debate about War</u> (2007) and published by the Georgetown University Press in Washington, D.C.12 In the next chapter, we shall examine <u>five</u> different kinds of revolutions.

Undeniably, war can be very traumatic, violent and a very terrible experience. I have personally experienced the effects of war during the Nigeria-Biafra War of 1967-1970. I hate war because of what it does to people and a country. However, at the same time, war is not always and necessarily a bad thing. You may remember that I wrote earlier that the Second World War was necessary because Adolf Hitler had to be stopped for the sake of human freedom.

In the Western world, they have developed what is called a "just war" tradition In 2007, David Kinsella and Craig L. Carr published a book titled <u>The Morality of War: A Reader</u>, and as this title suggests, the two authors examined the "when" and "why" about wars. They questioned whether wars should be fought at all.13

Some of you reading this will remember that in 1990, nineteen years ago, Priye Sunday Torulagha completed a doctoral dissertation on the moral norms regarding war in pre-colonial, traditional, Nigerian society. This was one investigation into the "just war" concept in an African context.

I believe that all discussions about war and morality should have a theological basis. I do not believe in the idea of "ethics-without-God."14

31

For, why should I be concerned about the effects of war on human society if I have no higher authority to whom I am accountable?

Therefore, in some limited circumstances, war may be redemptive and constructive, as the Bible indicates in many of its passages. Hence, war may be a good thing as in the case of the overthrow of Sodom and Gomorrah or the Third Reich, so as to maintain universal freedom on earth. Still, there may be some people in Africa who are absolutely opposed to revolution because they have been part of or the beneficiaries of the Establishment.

Being part of the Establishment which had oppressed the people, they are terribly frightened at the thought of a revolution because of any possible reprisals or negative consequences that will affect them. They know that those who had been oppressed and exploited for so long may one day be liberated and may seek revenge.15

Our attempt to develop a revolutionary theology should begin with a clear and proper understanding about the <u>character</u> of God, His attributes and our clarity on the subject of God as Creator and owner of the universe, including the planet we live in. We should not and cannot put God into an intellectual box and try to make Him fit into our preconceived ideas or conceptions of who He ought to be.

We must resist this kind of temptation, if we are to be honest. We must let God be God and let the Scriptures speak as it pleases. For the Christian, the Bible is a lamp to our feet and a light to our paths. The Bible is our guide for all matters of faith and life. Hence, our first discovery will be that God is not a Republican Party ideologue nor a Democrat. Neither is God a pacifist or a conscientious objector to war.

In the Bible, we do not see God sitting idly back, with His hands folded and beholding evil and the devil take on their courses of action. GOD HATES EVIL. Why? Because of His holy character. God is holy, utterly good, righteous and just. His attack upon evil and sin is not capricious but necessarily part of his nature.

God cannot and will not behold iniquity (Habakkuk 1:13). He does not acquit the evil doer, nor does He unjustly punish the righteous. He is always a just God whether we understand His ways or not. At the same time, He is LOVE, very compassionate, merciful, gracious, and longsuffering. There is none like our God.

THE BIBLE'S STANCE ON WAR

There are many references in the Bible on the subject of war and battles, just as there are many about peace. However, paradoxically, the Bible speaks about war and peace in the sense that they are both tools in God's providential actions. The author L. E. Toombs wrote that "the concept of the holy war, declared, led, and won by Yahweh himself, governs OT military thinking."16

Scripture tells us that "the LORD is a man of war" (Ex. 15:3). The prophet Joel exclaimed: "Prepare war, wake up the mighty men"(3:9). In the book of Numbers, we read these words: "If ye go to war in your land against the enemy that oppresseth you, then ye shall blow an alarm with the trumpets, and ye shall be remembered before the LORD your God, and ye shall be saved from your enemies" (10:9).

In 2 Chronicles 20:15, another prophet, Jahaziel declares: "for the battle is not yours, but God's." In these two texts of Scripture, we have the conditions under which Israel may go to war, the method to arouse their people to war, the connection of war to their theology and the victory which should follow after a war.

Also, an important point to remember is that God promised the Israelites a land flowing with milk and honey; but they had to fight before they could possess the land. Sometimes, nations must also fight in order to have their rights and freedoms. As Edmund Burke once put it, "the cause of freedom is the cause of God."

J. W. Wevers, in his writings, observed that in the Bible, springtime was the time of the year "when kings go forth to battle" (2 Sam. 11:1).17 In most biblical wars, the soldiers usually lived off the land of the enemy whose territory they had invaded. The nation of Israel for a long time probably had no well-paid, standing, army until the era of King Saul.

We can safely say that many great men and women in the Old Testament were military officers, including Abraham, Moses, Caleb, Joshua, Deborah, Samson, Jephtah, King Saul, King David, and King Hezekiah. In the New Testament, Cornelius was a Roman army officer. There were many early Christians within King Herod's army. Jesus did not reprove the Roman army officer who needed His help but held him high for his faith in Christ.

We should also remember that it was a Roman army officer who, at the foot of the Cross, testified that truly Jesus was the Son of God. Whether we believe he knew what he was saying or not, this confession is recorded in the Scriptures for a purpose. Therefore, the Bible is not anti-military. Rather, it admonishes soldiers not to extort nor exploit people because they carry the gun.

In their most recent book, <u>Battles of the Bible: A Military History of Ancient Israel</u>, Chaim Herzog and Mordecai Gichon provided an excellent work on the wars of ancient Israel.18 They argued that because of her strategic position in the Middle East, Israel had to maintain an efficient war machine in order to secure her freedom.

Herzog and Gichon, however, did not analyze the theological basis for Israel's wars. But there is no denial that at the battle and fall of Jericho, Joshua went to war at the direction of Yahweh who supplied the information on the war plan for victory.19

The ministry of Jesus Christ, however, seemed to have gone against the grain with regards to wars and military conquests. Again, the author L. E. Toombs observed that "war [was] ... not a central concern in the ministry of Jesus."20 The prophets had stated that Jesus would be the Prince of Peace. Why did He not use force or the power of war to achieve His aims? <u>Because He did not have to</u>. All power on Earth and in heaven were already within His reach.

At His trial, Jesus said to Pontius Pilate that he (Pilate) had no power to execute Him except that power was given to Pilate from heaven (John 19:11). And, at His arrest, Jesus demanded that Peter shield his sword because He (Jesus) had the power to call upon God to provide more than 80,000 fighting angels to defend Him (Mtt.26:53). Such angels had protected prophet Elisha from foreign attack, how much more would they protect Jesus!

As He had demonstrated during the Temptation in the wilderness, Jesus had access to angelic service. The earthly ministry of Jesus was not about a contest of powers or the use of force to accomplish His mission. He was a servant-messiah, not a political tyrant or despot (Mtt.20:28). This point should always be kept in mind by the followers of Jesus. Jesus was not anti-political, either.

I must reiterate that the Scriptures say that "the weapons of our warfare are not carnal but (nonetheless) mighty through God" (2 Cor. 10:4). In principle, God is not against war absolutely. In the book of Numbers 21:14, we read about the "book of the wars of the Lord." God can use wars to fulfill His divine purposes whether we like it or not. After all, God is a Sovereign King.

It is interesting to note that the term, Jehovah-Shalom, follows after the command to Gideon to militarily subdue the Midianites (Judges 6:24). God can use war to derive the best and greater good for His people. We should not forget that eventually a very sinful Israel was banished into the Babylonian and Assyrian captivity for hundreds of years. Finally, Israel ceased to exist as a nation from about 70 A.D. until 1948.

However, not all wars are as a result of God's initiative. I believe that a war to destroy the Earth is certainly against the declared will and purpose of God. Pogroms and genocides aimed at the glory and selfish desires of a tyrant do not come under God's penumbra.

Having said this much, the African should bear in mind the underlisted points that I am about to make. I really doubt whether President Abraham Lincoln would have made any progress in the matter of slavery had he chosen to be a pacifist while the twin evils of slavery and rebellion ravaged his country, the U.S. Also, I wonder if he had no theology of war in order to carry on the war efforts.

I also wonder if George Washington, the father of the American Republic, would have dared to face the might of the British military had he no theology of war during the Revolutionary war. From my readings, it is obvious that both Lincoln and Washington were men of faith, even if their faith may be described as deistic.

Therefore, I believe that those who seek to engage in revolutionary actions without the aid of God and faith in Him are usually doomed to failure. Such may momentarily seem to succeed but, in the long run, their revolutions will not stand.

We have seen this happen in the collapse of the Soviet Union, the Berlin Wall, Communism, and Fascism. Even communist China has had to make some political and economic adjustments in order to avert the possibility of internal divisions which can lead to a bloody revolution.

TOWARD AN AFRICAN REVOLUTIONARY THEOLOGY

The African ought to understand that God does not sanction all actions of the state. But, He does seem to endorse those policies which are redemptive and purposeful. He will crush the evil designs of men and women that attempt to destroy His good will. Herein must the

African seek divine wisdom and enlightenment when engaging in any revolutionary action.

The destinies of individuals and nations are involved in such actions. I am very persuaded to believe that Africans can model after the six-fold revolutionary ministry of Jesus as recorded in Luke 4:18. This passage reads as follows:

> The Spirit of the Lord is upon me, because he has anointed me to preach the gospel to the poor. He has sent me to heal the broken-hearted, to preach deliverance to the captives, and recovery of sight to the blind, to set at liberty them that are bruised, to preach the acceptable year of the Lord.

For the sake of clarity, let me reiterate what this six-fold ministry entails:

1. dealing with poverty, both natural and spiritual, elevating their condition. This is at the center of God's heart.
2. healing the sick, both physically and spiritually.
3. deliverance, that is, freedom from demonic operations; exorcism from Satanic domination and control.
4. recovery of sight, that is, dealing with physical and spiritual myopia; mental, emotional disorders and providing a vision for one's life. The Bible says that "where there is no vision, the people perish."
5. dealing with oppressive forces and setting the people free from them.
6. preaching, that is, declaring the Good News of God's love. This kind of six-fold ministry is both redemptive as it is revolutionary.

It is this kind of ministry that brings about fundamental changes to the fabric of society. In Acts 10:38, the Bible states that Jesus went about doing good, not evil. He was not destructive in any way. The Beatitudes recorded in Matthew 5 show that the message of Christ was revolutionary.

He would say something like this: "Previously, you had been taught so and so ... but I say ..." Christ did not ask people to imitate Him;

He asked those who would follow Him to be ready and willing to die, if necessary, for Him and His cause.

Christ's demands from us were nothing short of a revolutionary commitment. The African, particularly, the African Christian, should understand that the very word of God is powerful and revolutionary. God's words are no suggestions nor requests; they are commandments – they are the words of a King – and the Law for life.

In Hebrews 4:12, we read as follows:

> For the word of God is quick, and powerful than any two-edged sword, piercing even to the dividing asunder of soul and spirit, and of the joints and marrow, and is a discerner of the thoughts and intents of the heart.

The problem associated with the above text is that most of us do not really believe what it says. We come to it with our own mental attitudes and interpretations. We do not take it as it is. But, if we were to accept it on its face value and as the word of God, then, we would discover that it is talking about the revolutionary power of God which produces a transformation in men and women.

Here are some examples of the effect of the word of God: a prostitute becomes a decent man or woman; a thief stops to steal but restitutes; the thief begins to work for a living and shares his earnings with his neighbors. A murderer repents and is very willing to accept the responsibility for taking an innocent life. A sinner becomes a saint. The Bible says: "Therefore, if any man is in Christ, he becomes a new creature" (2 Corinth.5:17) This is the revolutionary effect of the word of God.

But, if the gospel does not possess this sort of quality and impact, it is useless, good for nothing, and has no distinctive merit to be called the word of God. The book of Jeremiah puts it bluntly: "Is not my word like a fire, declares the LORD, and like hammer that breaks a rock in pieces?" (23:29). In Hebrews 12:29, we read that "our God is a consuming fire."

This is the fiery element in the word of God which produces the revolutionary impact upon human beings. A Christian civilization, even Christianity, would never have lasted for more than 2,000 years had it not been for its revolutionary impact throughout all the ages.

Unlike other religions, Christianity does not win souls by the threat of a sword! We persuade men and women, not force them or kill them.

Additionally, the impact that the word of God has upon people is through the blessed Holy Spirit. We should never forget this point. A revolutionary theology implies that our God is not dead; He is very much alive. Neither is our God weak, as some suppose Him to be. He is strong and powerful. That is why He is called God Almighty.

God loves us but also hates evil and sin. How he is like that I cannot figure out. He loves the penitent and repentant soul very, very much. The courts of heaven are just and righteous. You can depend upon it. But, be very sure of this fact: Our Holy God will ultimately make war with His enemies. The Bible says: "The wicked shall be turned into hell, and the nations that forget God" (Ps. 9:17). There will be no negotiations with God!

In his book which we have cited frequently, Dr. Vernon C. Grounds offered a blueprint for doing a theology of revolution and here are eight ingredients for that kind of work:

1. Preaching the whole gospel for the whole man. Grounds wrote: "The simple fact of preaching the gospel is like putting sticks of dynamite into the social structure."21

2. Although secular governments may not take the implications of evangelistic, biblical preaching seriously, African ministers ought to understand that God is doing His great work through the gospel. This was one reason why St. Paul stated that he was not ashamed of **the gospel of Christ, for it is the power of God**.

3. The revision of the traditional modes or ways of doing Church work. The Church must totally and completely understand the revolutionary nature of the gospel and not be afraid to proclaim it. Like St. Peter of old, a minister of God should take a stand to obey God rather than men. Like Martin Luther, the German reformer, each minister should be able to say, "Here I stand."

4. Each believer in Christ should be taught to understand that authentic faith is really an instrument of liberation or freedom rather than one of repression and oppression. Christians ought to be the ones who are quick to set at liberty those that are bruised, following the example of the abolitionists and people

like John Brown in America. They should not be passive about tyranny and despotism.

The Christian Church should NEVER be on the side of the oppressor, exploiter and evil. Rather, the Church must always be a "confessing" Church, even if she is facing a billion Nazis, fascists or tyrants and despots in Africa.

5. The Church must NEVER change her biblical theology in order to suit any revolutionary idealism. On the contrary, any idealism must be made to conform with the gospel of Christ as led by His Holy Spirit.

6. There must always be a Christian hope because a world without hope tends to destroy itself through nihilism. Real hope is found in the eschatological teaching of the Scriptures. This kind of hope agrees with Aristotle who said that "the Good of man must be the Science of Politics."21 This kind of belief is in agreement with the will of God who desires that "it will be well with us" (Deut. 4:40; 5:29 and 33; 6:18).

7. If the African Church understands that it is the will of God that it goes well for them in this life, then, they should have nothing to fear. They should not be passive about making faith "the catalyst of authentic revolution."22 The term would no longer be a frightening, offensive word. They would embrace it as part of the vocabulary for doing God's will on Earth.

8. In the finality of life, we see Jesus as the King of Kings and Lord of Lords, who is crowned with honor and glory, as portrayed in the book of Revelation. He returns to Earth to judge in the New Millennium. His revolution reaches a climax when there is a new heaven and a new Earth. He then rules over His enemies for ever and ever.

It is here that the Church triumphant emerges to rule and reign with her King. This includes the African Church whose wars and battles with evil will have finally come to an end. She has fought the good fight and each of her obedient saints receives a crown reserved for those who have been faithful to the end as "more than conquerors." Even so, let that day come quickly, Lord Jesus.

CHAPTER FIVE
Five Kinds Of Revolutions

There are many kinds of revolutions. But, in this chapter, we want to consider only five: bloody, peaceful, quiet, ethical and a "Jesus" revolution. There can also be a scientific, intellectual, economic, technological, and an agrarian revolution. These lie outside the scope of this study.

In order for the African world revolution to succeed, I believe that each African revolutionary leader must thoroughly understand these various kinds of revolutions which we are to engage in. A person should not engage in a revolution foolishly. The process of a revolution could change from its original intent and lead thousands to their death.

A BLOODY REVOLUTION

A bloody revolution is one in which by definition much blood is spilled for its purpose to be accomplished. Proponents of this kind of revolution are Karl Marx, Mao Tse-tung, Joseph V. D. Stalin, Vladimir I. Lenin and all who shed blood in order to effect a social or political change. For these kinds of revolutionists, the end justifies the means.

The leaders of such a revolution tend to play God. They are the ones who pretend to know thoroughly or fully what is wrong with society and think that they have all the solutions to the problems of man. They rarely admit that they are capable of making mistakes or errors. Often self-conceited, they seldom would accept any opposition which must be crushed ruthlessly.

Karl Marx believed and predicted that in any successful class struggle among workers, there will be heaven on Earth. What we know as the Establishment or government would fade away. The dictatorship of the "proletariat" would emerge and replace the old order. Man would live in peace and harmony. This kind of reasoning is utopian.

But, in practice, we now know that "TEN MILLION people were killed to bring about collectivism in the Soviet Union."1 According to the reverend Dr. D. James Kennedy, "Stalin slaughtered more than forty million people."2

In Germany, Adolf Hitler believed in a revolution that would spill much blood to create his Aryan empire. He learned very well from Lenin, whom Kennedy referred to as "the father of the modern totalitarian state."3 So, Hitler began by killing the Jews, Gypsies, Slavs, Poles, and anyone else whom the Nazis deemed to be racially inferior.

According to James Kennedy, "the first victims of the Holocaust were 70,000 insane and 'incurable' people. But in the end, 6 million Jews and 9-10 million others, many of whom were Christians were murdered."4 Chairman Mao believed that in order for his so-called cultural revolution in China to succeed, China had to do away with her past.

Mao's biographers, Jung Chang and Jon Halliday tell us:

> When he [Mao] came to the question 'How do we change [China?]' Mao laid the utmost emphasis on destruction ... the country must be destroyed and then reformed. He extended this line not just to China but to the world – and even the universe. This applies to the country, to the nation, and to mankind... The destruction of the universe is the same. 'People like me long for its destruction, because when the old universe is destroyed, a new universe will be formed. Isn't that better!'5

Mao was only 24 years old when he made the above declaration which remained the core of his philosophy of life. Years later, when he acquired power, this line of thinking led ultimately to the elimination of the intellectuals, Communists and all who dared to oppose him, including his own Chinese people. According to James Kennedy, "Mao was responsible for killing about 72 million human beings."6

In the first ten years of Mao's rule, that is, from 1948 to 1958, 24.7 million people were slaughtered. Between 1959 and 1962, 25 million more people were murdered. And, from 1969 to 1976, an additional 22 million people were killed, a total of about 72 million human lives.7 This was the price for the Chinese revolution.

In Africa, there have also been some scoundrels who experimented with a bloody so-called revolution that involved the destruction of human lives. A total of 5.7 million people have perished from senseless killings since independence in 1960. For example, Francisco Marcias Nguema is alleged to have murdered 50,000 people in Equatorial Guinea during his regime.

In Uganda, Idi Amin was notorious for the slaughter of 800,000 people. In Ethiopia, Marian Mengistu was responsible for the death of 150,000 people. In 1994 in Rwanda, 800,000 people perished from the massacres there. As we read these lines, more than 300,000 people have perished in the Darfur region in the Sudan, Arab Moslems are killing Black and African Moslems at the instigation of the regime there. This is revolution Sudanese style.

What can we say of the killings in the Democratic Republic of the Congo, in Burundi, in Zimbabwe, in Nigeria where, in the Civil War of 1967 to 1970, over two million people died needlessly. Nigerian leaders have learned absolutely nothing from that tragedy! Was it a revolution or not?

But, these were attempts toward changes, if ever they were, at the terrible price of many innocent and precious human lives. Generally, the victims had no clue as to what was going on. Many were innocent civilians unschooled in revolutionary drama.

Therefore, African leaders must seriously weigh and consider what kind of revolution they want. The question must be asked: "Do we want a bloody revolution and at what price? Would it be worth it? Who will bear the cost of the revolution? For how long will it last?" These questions lead us to consider the next alternative.

A Peaceful Revolution

At once, some critic will say that there is nothing peaceful about any revolution. Such a critic has obviously skipped the reading of Chapter One of this book. But, in 1963, Betty Schechter, born and raised in the city of New York, a graduate of Smith College in 1942, authored an important book which she titled, <u>The Peaceable Revolution</u>.8

Schechter examined and analyzed the views and actions of Henry David Thoreau, Mohandas Gandhi and Martin Luther King, Jr. with regard to the theory of non-violence as an instrument for socio-political change. The practice of non-violence has been considered an alternative to a bloody revolution.

In modern times, non-violent civil disobedience was first initiated by Thoreau (1817-1862).9 But the concept seems to have been practiced by the early Christian apostles as in the case when St. Peter and his colleagues chose prison sentence rather than cease to preach the gospel (Acts 4:18 and 5:28-32).

A graduate of Harvard University in 1837, and one of the most influential persons in American thought, Thoreau was a supreme individualist. He championed the cause of the human spirit against materialism and social conformity.

He moved out of Concord, Massachusetts, his town of birth to a lakeshore community called Walden Pond, to be close to nature and to study and write about it. He built himself a small cabin and his life and experiences there later became the subject of his most famous book, Walden, which was published in 1854 at the age of 37.

One day, in July 1846, Thoreau was arrested for refusing to pay a poll tax, a tax he believed was in furtherance of the U.S. – Mexican War of 1846-1848. Thoreau spent a night in jail, claiming to be a conscientious objector to a war he believed was an effort to extend slavery into a foreign territory.

In 1849, he published an essay titled, "Resistance to Civil Government," in order to defend his position. Thoreau was fully aware of the principles of freedom and revolution enunciated in the slogan, "no taxation without representation." Thus, he withheld payment of the taxes. His idea was to withhold that which was due to the state.

Thoreau argued that,

> All men recognize the right of revolution, that is, the right to refuse allegiance to, and to resist, the government, when its tyranny or its inefficiency are great and unendurable.10

Before the end of his life, Thoreau had become a member of the Underground Railroad, the organization which assisted American slaves to emigrate into Canada. He died of tuberculosis on May 6, 1862, at the young age of 45. He was a prolific writer whose varied ideas covered twenty volumes of books when they were published in 1906.

Thoreau was a forerunner whose ideas would influence such great world leaders like Gandhi of India and Martin Luther King, Jr., of the United States. Gandhi, a young man who was born on October 2, 1869, in "a small, seaside town ... in western India,"11 studied law in England. Upon his return in 1891, he settled first in South Africa, hoping to practice law there and to make a career in law.

However, Gandhi devoted himself to a life of selfless sacrifice for his people. Consequently, he was often persecuted by the apartheid regime, abused and physically assaulted several times, but was ready to die for his beliefs and actions. During the years of 1891 and 1914, he was often incarcerated.

In her book, Schechter stated that it was while in prison in South Africa that Gandhi read Thoreau's "Civil Disobedience" and "was deeply impressed." She added: "Already a peaceable rebel against a repressive government, Mohandas Gandhi, an Indian, found new inspiration in the words of the rebel of Concord, Massachusetts."12 Gandhi incorporated Thoreau's ideas of peaceful resistance into the philosophy of his own life.

Gandhi was also influenced by the vegetarianism of the Fabian Society during his time in England. But as a devotee to Hinduism, he found strength in the ahimsa doctrine within his religion. Ahimsa taught him not to do any harm or injury to anyone. Of ahimsa, Gandhi said that there was no limit to its power.13 He read other books by Leo Tolstoy, John Ruskin, William Morris and Edward Arnold.

Gandhi loved the ethical principles of Jesus as expressed in the Sermon on the Mount but he was confused about the Old Testament. He personally read the Bible and his readings assisted him to develop his philosophy of satyagrapha or truth-force (soul-force). This philosophy was rooted in his religious convictions, including Christianity. He called it his experiment with Truth,

Gandhi's experiment was actually "an active and open resistance to evil and injustice without resort to violence, while simultaneously, attempting both to perfect one's own self-control and to convert the opponent to the cause of justice."14 Satyagrapha was first developed in South Africa but was ultimately applied fully in the anti-colonial struggles of India against British imperialism.

As a practical measure, Gandhi advocated boycotts and strikes. In 1935, he predicted that "it may be through the Negroes that the unadulterated message of nonviolence will be delivered to the world."15 This prediction came to pass through the message of Dr. Martin Luther King, Jr.

But, sadly, on January 30, 1948, the year that the modern state of Israel was born, this apostle of nonviolence was violently mistreated. Gandhi was assassinated while on his way to pray. The world stood still to take note of his great contributions to modern civilization. India had gained her independence from Britain the year before Gandhi's death.

Gandhi showed the world that <u>revolutions did not always have to be bloody</u>. On February 10, 1959, nearly eleven years after the death of Gandhi, the young African American preacher, Martin Luther King, Jr., visited India, the country of his mentor, to study more about <u>satyagrapha</u> and to use it in his struggles during the Civil Rights Movement of the 1960s in the U.S.

Dr. King, Jr. was born on January 15, 1929, which was during the years of the Great Depression in the U.S. He came from a family of black preachers. He was educated at Morehouse College from 1944 to 1948 and, thereafter, attended Crozer Theological Seminary located at Chester, Pennsylvania. He obtained his doctorate degree from Boston University in 1953 at the age of 24.

Although he followed after the family's occupation as a preacher, fate brought King, Jr. into the role of a nonviolent revolutionary and visionary leader who sought socio-political changes for Americans, particularly, the African Americans.

In December 1955, two years after his graduation, the now famous Bus boycott in Alabama, resulting from Mrs. Rosa Parks' arrest for refusing to give up her seat in a public bus to a white person, brought King to national and international attention. King, Jr. was only 26 at the time.

He had "dreams of helping the Negro people."16 He had a vision that one day, his young children would no longer be judged by the color of their skin, but by the content of their character. He had dreams of better days ahead for his people. But, at the time, white America was steeped in racism, segregation, Jim Crow and all other kinds of social, political and economic injustices. The odds seemed heavily against King's people.

Obviously, there were some people who believed that only a bloody revolution could bring the necessary changes. But King, Jr. understood the military might of white Americans, just as Gandhi had also understood the military power of the British Empire. This military option implied racial suicide. Were blacks ready for another Masada?

King was undaunted. Change had to come somehow. Therefore, he placed implicit faith and confidence in the principles of the nonviolent social action which had worked well in India. I believe that his faith was rooted in his Christian upbringing and in the Scriptures.

For King, nonviolence was a way of life, not just a method of resistance. King's nonviolence came to be expressed in six basic aspects, namely:

1. Nonviolence is not a way of life for cowards.
2. Nonviolence does not seek to defeat or humiliate the enemy, but to win his friendship and understanding.
3. The attack is directed against the forces of evil and <u>not</u> against the perpetrators of evil.
4. Nonviolence involves a willingness to accept suffering without retaliation.
5. Nonviolence avoids not only external physical violence but also an internal violence of the spirit. There must be no hatred for the opponent.
6. Nonviolence is based on the conviction that the universe is on the side of justice. There is faith and hope in the future.17

King was fully aware that the protests by his people in the 1955 Bus boycott and thereafter could spill over into terrible violent demonstrations and deaths for which he would be held responsible. But, being a gifted public speaker, he managed well the crowds by his personal attitude, charisma, discipline and immense courage.

By 1963, his fame and leadership were recognized when he gave the "I HAVE A DREAM" speech in Washington, D.C., to a crowd of about 250,000 people. Barack Obama, the first black person to become the 44th president of the United States, would exceed that number in 2008.

King's speech became one of the classical orations of the modern world. He also organized many "Freedom Rides" and demonstrations. He opposed the unpopular Vietnam War. He constantly faced the possibility of a white lynch mob and death. Once, in New York city, he came quite close to death when he was stabbed by a woman. He wrote that if he had just sneezed on that occasion, he would have died!18

But, he persevered and persisted. In 1964, the world gave full recognition to his efforts when he received the Nobel Peace Prize at the age of 35. Sadly, four years later, on April 4, 1968, the 39-year-old peaceful revolutionary was murdered. He was shot on the balcony of the Lorraine Motel in Memphis, Tennessee, while standing and talking to his colleagues. America turned around to honor her great son by the dedication of a national holiday to King's birth every January 15th.

The positive results of the Civil Rights Movement, which the reverend Dr. Martin Luther King, Jr. spearheaded, are many and may even today be taken for granted by many young people. But, barely 50 years ago, many places in America, such as some theatres, restaurants, public transportation, schools and even some churches and cemeteries, were inaccessible to African Americans. "For Whites Only" signs were noticeable everywhere.

Racial profiling was the order of the time and inter-racial marriages were considered taboo and were frowned at. The lynching of a black man was very possible just for winking at a white woman. False accusations of rape by a white woman against a black man were frequent. Many of these things were gradually eradicated by the peaceful revolution led by King and we owe him a lot of gratitude. The King legacy continues.

A QUIET REVOLUTION

Two authors have provided me with the inspiration to discuss this third kind of revolution. They are John Perkins, author of A Quiet Revolution (1976) and Fantu Cheru, who authored the book, The Silent Revolution in Africa (1993).

Perkins was the late evangelical and radio broadcaster of the "Voice of Calvary" in Jackson, Mississippi. Perkins's book dealt with strategies for a Christian response to human need today. Like many emerging leaders, Perkins was born into abject poverty, with no silver spoon in his mouth. One of eight children in a Mississippi sharecropper's family, Perkins dropped out of school in the third grade.

At the age of 17, he traveled to California in search of opportunities which were denied him in his own state. He became a Christian, worked very hard and rose to the level of a national spokesman and a board member of many institutions, including the Ford Foundation. He wrote his book on revolution in order to answer the question: "What will change the lives of the poor people of America?"19

Perkins's answer to his question was "a quiet revolution," not one that looked for a pie in the sky in the bye and bye, but one that dealt with the concrete realities of life here and now. The Church, he wrote, "had to deal with the social and economic structures that oppressed the people."20 In the last chapter of his book, which he titled, "A Quiet Revolution Through the Church," Perkins emphatically insisted that: "We need a quiet revolution."21

Perkins cited former U. S. Senator, Mark Hatfield of Oregon who, in reference to revolution, had said that,

> What will be required is what has always been most difficult to accomplish without violence: a redistribution of power, and the wealth that brings power, an end to preemption of resources by the rich; and a replacement for the kind of economics which divides the world.22

Optimistically, Perkins added: "I see with hope that God is beginning a quiet revolution in his church."23 He went on to explain how one can become a part of the quiet revolution, as follows:24

1. relocating the Body of Christ among the poor and in the areas of need
2. reconciliation across racial and cultural barriers, and,
3. redistribution of wealth.

"If the blood of injustice is economics," Perkins argued, then, "we must as Christians seek justice by coming up with means of redistributing goods and wealth to those in need."25 This was a call to radical economic transformation . He asserted that doing this was biblical and a Christian mandate of the quiet revolution. This proposition, in reality, sounded very naïve since, in America, capitalistic Christians would find this call very hard to comply with.

Dr. Fantu Cheru is a Professor of Development Studies in the School of International Service at the American University in Washington, D.C. While Perkins's **quiet revolution** was addressed to American Christians, Cheru's **silent revolution** analyzed and examined the African economic situation.

Cheru rejected the Western economic prescriptions as "blueprints for the recolonization of Africa."26 This was a serious accusation. But, Cheru praised the efforts of ordinary Africans who opted out of the formal market to develop a parallel barter economy impervious to the machinations of their rulers and the International Monetary Fund (IMF).

This domestic economic approach was at the center of Cheru's silent revolution in Africa. Clearly, both Perkins and Cheru believed that a quiet or silent revolution was in the making both in the African diaspora and on the continent. It was to be a revolution that would uplift black Americans as well as Africans, **without resorting to violence and unnecessary bloodshed**.27

From hindsight, the problem with this revolutionary process is that it may be too slow to emancipate the poor. History has shown that the rich often do not easily give up their cherished wealth and acquisitions, for redistribution, without a fight. But, let us consider our fourth alternative for a revolution.

AN ETHICAL REVOLUTION

In Chapter Three of this book, I discussed the necessity for a revolution in Africa, particularly, in the realm of ethics and morality. Ethics has been defined as "the study of moral conduct," while morality is said to be "the conduct and codes of conduct of individuals and groups."28 Moral judgments relate to the actual actions of human beings insofar as they are considered right or wrong.

For any concrete and meaningful change to occur in Africa, it is my position that there must equally be a revolution in the area of morals and ethics. Africans have to do more work in the area of ethical and moral philosophy. If Africa is to survive as an entity, as a people, then there must be a revolution of African morality and ethics.

With the current levels of corruption and moral decay in African societies, our political collapse is imminent. Traditionally, our morals and ethics were rooted in our culture. Our values were expressed through our culture and spirituality. In many parts of Africa, such values were our unwritten codes of conduct.

For example, a thief knew exactly what punishment awaited him or her if they were caught. Murders of innocent people were rare since there was respect for human life. Our respect for elders and veneration of the ancestors were not encoded into a written law like the Hebrew Ten Commandments. But, everyone knew and understood what was taboo, outrageous, blasphemous and sacrilegious.29

There were no lawyers who twisted the law and allowed criminals to go guiltless. Our young people learned at home what was right or wrong and what were the expected norms of behavior. No child dared to curse the parents! Truth was known and lies were lies. Then came capitalism and the so-called Western morals and ethics branded as civilization.

Africa lost her sense of order, morality and ethics to the extent that life has become very cheap and moneymania has replaced all sense of decency. In the name of modernity, many of our people dress without shame and no blushing. According to Chinua Achebe, things have really fallen apart in Africa. Even a four-year-old can curse the parents. At 14, they can't wait to leave home and parade their girl or boy "friends" who often seem to be more honorable than their parents. They call all this freedom!

Africa has lost much in the clash of cultures. Hence, there is a desperate need for a thorough re-definition of the African ethical and moral position. I believe that this is one reason why Nigeria is "rebranding" herself. We must halt the descent into moral anarchy and ethical myopia.

We know that the Western world has had a long tradition of ethical scholarship. One of their scholars writes that "ethical philosophy began in the fifth century B.C. with the appearance of Socrates, a secular prophet ..."30 This is nonsensical thinking since Africans know that this statement is partly a wrong generalization.

The African empires, kingdoms and dynasties which predated Greece and Rome did not wallow in ethical ignorance or stupidity until the emergence of the Romans and the Greeks. From Socrates to the intrusion of the West into African life in 1415, there was no <u>tabula rasa</u> in African notions of morality and ethics. For instance, the ancient Egyptians had their code of ethics.

The Code of Hammurabi existed before the Greeks and Romans appeared.

The late Jerry Falwell, the founder of Liberty University, used to say that law is legislated morality. The Hebrews had their moral code, the Ten Commandments. And, the Chinese had theirs through the thoughts of Confucius. The Western school of ethical scholarship have many notable names.

Such names include Socrates (469-399 B.C.) whose ethical ideas were given to us through his disciple, Plato (428-348 B.C.), author of the book, <u>The Republic</u>. Aristotle's ethical ideas came to us through his book, <u>Nicomachean Ethics</u>.

It is said that Aristotle (384-322 B.C.) "wrote the first really systematic treatise on ethics."31 But how did the ancient Egyptians in Africa exist from 3100-1087 B.C. (over two thousand years) without any ethical and moral formulations? Bear in mind that writing first appeared in Egypt around 3150 B.C., according to the historian Henri-Jean Martin.

Thomas Acquinas represented the medieval school of Western ethical thought. Immanuel Kant authored four important books on ethics: <u>The Foundations of Morals</u>; <u>Critique of Pure Reason</u>; <u>Critique of Practical Reason</u> ; and <u>Critique of Judgment</u>.

William Paley (1743-1805) wrote <u>Principles of Moral and Political Philosophy</u>, "a handbook on the duties and obligations of civil life," according to Elmer Sprague, while David Hume (1711-1776) wrote <u>An Enquiry Concerning the Principles of Morals</u> in 1751.

Jeremy Bentham (1748-1832) and John Stuart Mill (1806-1873) represented the utilitarian school of ethics, with slight differences between them Both men upheld "the greatest happiness" principle. But it was Immanuel Kant who established the ethical standard known as the "I ought" idea or "the categorical imperative" principle.

Kant believed that there was an objective moral law in the universe and that every time someone said, "I ought" to do this or that, such a person signified the existence of a moral obligation. But, at the turn of the 20th century, George Edward Moore (1873-1958), through his book,

Principia Ethica (1903), became the "starting point of contemporary ethical theory"32 in the Western world.

Other contemporary Western ethicists include Soren Kierkegaard, George Santayana, C. E. M. Joad and Sissela Bok, author of the book, Lying: Moral Choice in Public and Private Life, published in 1978. Western ethicists believe that ethics is the study of values in human conduct.33

"To ignore the role of values is to have a very distorted or one-sided view of man and his world."34 Values deal with what is to be man in the fullest meaning of the word. It is a matter of goodness and wrongness in human relations.

In the West, morality comes from the Latin word moralis. Ethics comes from the Greek term ethos while the Latin word rectus stands for right or straight. Also, both moralis and ethos mean a "way of life."35 "Morality grows out of life itself."36 Jesus gave to the Church the doctrine of the Golden Rule: do unto others as you would want others to do unto you. We wonder what words stand for morality and ethics in Africa. The Ibibio word for conduct or behavior is "ido."

There are three main approaches to ethical discourse in the Western world, namely:

1. the appeal to authority, a kind of going by the book or an ethical standard. For example, a Christian ethical position would refer to the Bible as its standard.
2. an appeal to ethical relativism and subjectivism. This view says that there are no ethical absolutes and that what is ethically or morally proper for one man or situation may be wrong or improper for another person.
3. an appeal to the situation. This is a modification of the second view above. It is the selection and application of ethics and morality to any given situation. Professor Joseph Fletcher (1905-1991), the great apostle of this school of thought, represents the new morality in Western ethics.

Along with the new morality are hedonism, Epicureanism and the "if it feels good, do it" philosophies. These are the new philosophies of pleasure and entertainment which dominate the perspectives of young Americans in matters of sexual gratification.

We may also add to the above considerations the values of freedom (which is becoming more and more of a license to do whatever), human and civil rights and nonviolence. Presently, a large segment of the Western world is claiming homosexuality and lesbianism as human rights! Hence, same-sex marriages are on the ascendancy. The old order of marriage as the union of man and woman is on its way out of vogue.

Still, many people do believe that there are absolute and intrinsic values and that the rule of law is central to political ethics. Without such absolute values – like truth, justice, freedom and peace – human society as we know it would crumble. Hence, laws, representing legislated morality, are made to protect a society from decay and self-destruction. Africa today needs the practice and permanence of good moral values and ethics.

Below are some of the ethical issues that confront Westerners today:

1. War and peace
2. Over-population
3. Global terrorism and neo-colonialism
4. Pre-emptive military actions
5. Resource control and conservation
6. Euthnasia
7. Hedonism
8. Secular humanism.

In my opinion, Africans today have no great ethicists of international repute since the field of study does not pay very well in terms of salary. I stand to be corrected. And, yet there are great ethical and moral issues and problems which daily confront the African and their governments. Some of these are:

1. kleptocracy and capital flight out from Africa
2. resource control and equitable redistribution
3. healthcare
4. fair and equitable taxation
5. relevant and functional education
6. efficient public service

7. equity and justice in award of public contracts
8. land reforms and adequate compensation
9. lying in public and private affairs
10. bribery and corruption
11. child trafficking and sexual abuses
12. domestic abuses and molestation

It is my belief that the African intellectuals (including those in the churches and mosques) are the ones responsible for providing the moral and ethical roadmap regarding the issues listed above. They must bring a peaceful moral revolution needed to turn the continent around. But if the intellectuals themselves are corrupt, too, to whom will the ordinary African turn to? The answer may not be sweet but the masses will turn to a bloody revolution.

A JESUS REVOLUTION

In his most useful book, in my opinion, The Revolt of the Masses (1993), first published in 1930, Jose Ortega y Gasset (1883-1955). provided a reason why an alternative revolution, even a "Jesus revolution," should be considered.

One of the intellectual leaders of the Spanish Republican government, Gasset wrote that "European civilization, I have repeated more than once, has automatically brought about the rebellion of the masses."37 He went further to show how this phenomenon came to pass,

Gasset concluded that "Europe has been left without a moral code," and he added: "I absolutely deny that there exists today in any corner of the continent a group inspired by a new ethos which shows signs of being a moral code."38

He made the statement during the inter-war years and I wonder what he would have said today about the Western moral code in the post-Iraqi and Afghanistan wars. For many people in the world, these wars have nearly destroyed Western (especially American) moral leadership and credibility.

For the survival of the world, we need a new code of ethics and morality. We also need a nonviolent revolution that is truly redemptive. I believe that it is only in the revolutionary message of Jesus Christ that such a revolution can be found. It is in His message that this sick, old, sinful world can find peace and redemption without resorting to bloodiness and violence.

Now, I know that some critic may say that Christianity has led to more wars than any other religion. Where is the evidence? I am not talking about <u>churchianity</u>, let alone the organized forms of the Church. I am painfully aware of the role of the Crusaders in Western civilization.

That role is no different from stating a blasphemy that Christopher Columbus was the saint who brought the Gospel to America! It would also be an insult to say that the arch-imperialist, Frederick Lugard, was the missionary who brought Christianity to Nigerians.

What I mean is that the message of Jesus Christ is different from much of what is done today in His name. His message is still redemptive, nonviolent, peaceful and powerful. Jesus Christ is alive and well and He is still in the business of transforming lives. Halleleuia.

The new morality of the Western world is quite confusing. While the West taught the Africans about the rules of the sovereignty of nations; while she claims that her history is rooted in the Christian ethics of love, peace and forgiveness; one finds little comfort or truth in the belligerence and arrogance of the West against weaker nations. That the West is always able to rationalize and justify her actions is no convincing defense to many Africans.

Africans do not forget that it was the West that gave to us two world wars. It was in the West that the Holocaust occurred. In many of the wars of the last and this new century, the West was neither provoked nor attacked first except for the 9/11 attack in 2001. Add to these wars the exploitative and hurtful aspects of capitalistic materialism!

However, the West is still loved by many Africans; but her morality and ethics still confuse many people abroad. Her decadence paraded as virtue is actually nauseating. Therefore, it is imperative that the Africans consider another kind of revolution as they cannot emulate the West in this respect.

When, in the year 2000, I published my book, <u>What's So Good About Christianity? Five Amazing Ways the Gospel Has Influenced and Blessed Our Lives</u>, I implicitly held the view that the **Gospel** (I did not say Christianity) has had a revolutionary impact upon our world.

Indeed, Dr. Billy Graham and many other world leaders would agree with me.

Graham pointed to the 1970s when America witnessed what Time magazine and the other media networks like NBC and CBS termed "the Jesus revolution." Graham dates 1971 as the exact year of the revolution. He called the youths of that era "the Jesus Generation."39 A similar, national movement occurred in Nigeria at that time, also.

Millions of young people experienced spiritual conversions which were authentic and genuine. They changed from the lifestyle of violence, drug addictions, alcoholism, decadence and rebellion to commitment to Jesus Christ. Many people noticed the change and so did the media. Great evangelists emerged from their ranks and modern man has been blessed by their ministries.

But, currently, we are at the crossroads for a new movement that will usher in another nonviolent change for good. Either we have this or a bloody revolution. Kirk Franklin, the African American music artist asked, "Do you want a revolution?" My answer is, yes, yes!

Vernon C. Grounds, cited often in this book, added further illumination to this idea of a Jesus revolution. Writing in a chapter he titled, "Jesus the Revolutionary," Dr. Grounds presented "the case for a Christian radicalism."40 He examined and analyzed the development of this concept by drawing his insights from the expert research of many scholars such as Oscar Cullman, Colin Morris (whom he quoted profusely) and S. G. F. Brandon, author of Jesus and the Zealots (1967).

Also, Grounds examined the work by R. F. Aldwinckle, a former systematic theologian, and agreed with these scholars that there are indications in the New Testament which can be interpreted to show that Jesus approximated the status of a political revolutionary, in line with the Jewish zealots of His day. And, it should never be forgotten that Jesus was crucified by the Romans for insurrection.

However, and indeed, Jesus was much more than a political insurrectionist. According to Oscar Cullman, "Jesus was no Zealot ... but His whole ministry was in continuous contact with Zealotism."41 Hence, Grounds concluded his analysis with this insight:

> Jesus Christ was the greatest revolutionary. But His revolution
> was not inaugurated and cannot be implemented by armed

violence, whether guns or sticks or atom bombs. It can be implemented only by the power which inaugurated His revolutionary kingdom, the power of suffering love.42

I ought to add that the power which Dr. Grounds spoke of is the power of the Holy Spirit who transforms the inner man. Also, it should be clear that the peaceful, quiet/silent and ethical revolutions can draw their inspirations from the Jesus revolution. Gandhi and King, Jr. did and they were not ashamed to do so. According to St. Paul, we should not be ashamed of the Gospel of Christ, for **it is the power of God** unto salvation (Rom. 1:16).

I have deliberately shied away from treatment of the African Islamic revolutionary theology since I have no expertise in that subject and it is likely to have been well documented in other books.43 Moreover, as author Robert Payne contended in his 1990 publication, Islam came to the world by the "Holy Sword" and the "Holy Word."44

Africans have to make the choice between the five kinds of revolutions presented here. It is my prayer that they will choose the right revolutionary path or perish. Furthermore, they can learn some lessons from the six historical revolutions discussed in the next two chapters. Read on.

CHAPTER SIX
Learning From Hebrew, English & American Revolutions

Surely, throughout the course of human history, there have been many revolutions. But here, we'll be focusing on discussing three major revolutions which have impacted our world the most and which also seem to be most significant. These three revolutions are the Hebrew, English and the American revolutions.

In chapter Seven, we shall focus on the French, Russian and Chinese revolutions. Because I believe that decolonization was Africa's first modern revolution, we shall discuss that issue in Chapter Eight. Before the end of this book, we shall examine how we ought to prepare ourselves for the coming African Revolution.

THE HEBREW OR JEWISH REVOLUTION

About eleven years ago, author Thomas Cahill published a captivating, persuasive and interesting book which he titled, The Gifts of the Jews: How A Tribe of Desert Nomads Changed the Way Everyone Thinks and Feels.1 He could have called his book, "The First Freedom: God's Revolutionary Gift to the World Through the Jewish People," because that is what the book is about.

For, until 1250 B.C., never was it heard, nor found anywhere else in all of recorded history, that a bunch of 600,000 slaves, after over 400 years of captivity, suddenly emancipated themselves wholly by divine fiat, without their slave masters successfully fighting back to retain their slaves.2

The story of the Hebrew or Jewish revolution sounds almost mythical, fictional, or incredible. The miracle of the birth of the Hebrew nation is that they ever left Egypt, broke away from the Egyptian empire, to form their own separate and independent nation. So great were the odds against the Hebrews that any such plot or attempt, without supernatural aid, would have been considered futile or suicidal.

In his book, <u>Power and Powerlessness in Jewish History</u> (1986), David Biale wrote that "the Jews were a remarkably contentious people in antiquity and developed a well-deserved reputation for military prowess." He added: "Not content to submit to the demands of their imperial masters, they repeatedly revolted in attempts to win full independence."3

And, how did these Hebrews (later known as the Jews) emerge from slavery to freedom to become such a reputable nation? Their story is told in a familiar book called the Bible. It is the story of the Exodus, the account of their very first revolution. This story can also be found in many other popular extra-biblical literature.

The Hebrew patriarchs were Abraham, Isaac and Jacob. Abraham, whose father was known as Terah, came from a city called Ur of the Chaldeans in the present-day Iraq. In his book, <u>God Spake by Moses</u> (1951), Professor Oswald T. Allis claimed that the Exodus was "the thrilling story of how God delivered Jacob's descendants from Egyptian bondage."4

Jacob and his family, third generation descendants of Abraham, had gone into Egypt as free immigrant people. They went there at the invitation of Joseph, one of the sons of Jacob, who had been thought dead but actually had been sold into slavery by his own brothers. They sold him out of envy because their father favored him. Moreover, Jacob and his family were fleeing from a famine that was ravaging their Canaanite settlement.

The precise date of their arrival into Egypt is unknown. But many scholars, including Cahill, have speculated that the journey was made prior to 1300 B.C. Professor Allis stated that the caravan which brought Jacob into Egypt "may have numbered 1,000 souls, perhaps considerably more."5 Within the Bible, in Acts 7:14, the number given is 75. But, in Genesis 46: 27, the figure is 70.

It is likely that the number was closer to 70 than 1,000, a figure which would have meant that the 12 children of Jacob each had 83 or 84 children. When we remember that King Ahab had 70 children, then it is not a far-fetched idea that a greater number than 70 came to Egypt. It also implies that Jacob's children each had about six children or more.

Cahill believed that Egypt was ruled by a Pharaoh called Set I, between 1304 B.C. and 1290 B.C., "the likely Pharaoh 'who knew not Joseph' and enslaved the Children of Israel."6 Cahill also contended that Ramses II was likely the Pharaoh who ruled Egypt between 1290 B.C. and 1224 B.C. According to Cahill's chronology, the Exodus (Hebrew Revolution) occurred about 1250 B.C.7

Allis, however, disputes the argument that Ramses II or even Set I ever enslaved the Hebrews. His opinion is that Thothmes III "may have been the Pharaoh who 'knew not Joseph' and oppressed the children of Israel."8 The historian Walther Kirchner believed that the Hebrews left Egypt about 1300 B.C. to invade Palestine.9

Whether these dates are accurate or not is not as important as the fact that there was a historical leader of the Hebrew Revolution whom we now know as Moses, an indispensable visionary leader. The Jews know him as Moshe (He-who-Pulls-Out).10 In his book, <u>Moses on Management</u> (1999), David Baron calls him "the greatest manager of all time, ... a liberator, law-giver, and intercessor par excellence ... a highly complex individual."11

Moses was born about 1210 B.C. and died about 1330 B.C. His father's name was Amram and his mother was Jochebed. Moses was the youngest of Amram's three children. The others were Aaron, an older brother and Miriam, his only sister. Due to the harsh decree of the ruling Pharaoh, Moses was born under a cloud of infanticide.

He grew up as the adopted son of the daughter of the Pharaoh of the time who raised him as her own son in the royal palace. Moses was "learned in all the wisdom of the Egyptians ... mighty in words and in deeds" (Acts 7: 22). The ruling Pharaoh had decreed that all the children at the time Moses was born be put to death because of the threat of the increasing numbers of Hebrew people. Therefore, Moses was hidden by his parents until he was discovered by Pharaoh's daughter in a river.

The editor of the volume, <u>A History of the Jewish People</u> (2002),

H. H. Ben-Sasson, claimed that extra-biblical sources are silent about Jacob's migration into Egypt, but that some Egyptian sources were "enlightening." He added that "in all likelihood, ... Ramses II should be regarded as the Pharaoh who oppressed the Israelites and during whose long reign they may have left Egypt."12

Ben-Sasson, who also appears to have believed that the Exodus actually occurred, stated that for the Jews, "the tradition of redemption ... became a cornerstone of their faith not only in the Pentateuch and the historiographic books of the Bible but also in the writings of the Prophets."13 The Jewish people were constantly warned NEVER to forget the miracle at the Red Sea, that is, the great liberation and emancipation by their God – Yahweh.

As if contending with those who might disagree with him, Ben-Sasson pointed to three other factors regarding the Exodus, namely:

1. the Egyptian border officials who were stationed at the Sinai frontier could have foiled any escape.
2. the pleas by Aaron and Moses for permission for the Hebrews to leave Egypt would have alerted Pharaoh of their plots to escape.
3. the suggestion that the Jews fled under cover of "the dead of night" was untenable since there were Egyptian boundary fortifications. In any case, how would 600,000 ex-slaves have escaped at night with all the noises and commotion from all their cattle, children and women? Such "stealing away" would have been impracticable.

Ben-Sasson also pointed to the towering position of Moses, a Levite, lawgiver, judge, and commander-in-chief, and noted how the God of the patriarchs progressively became the God of Moses, of Israel, and of all mankind, particularly, of those who believe. The influence of Moses upon world history was established by his authorship of the <u>Decalogue</u>, also known as the Ten Commandments, which has influenced much of the world ever since his time.

Not everyone seems convinced that the Exodus was orchestrated by an act of God. But the argument or case against it is weak. Paul Johnson, in his book, <u>A History of the Jews</u> (1988), wrote that "So far as we know, in fact, the Israelite-Hebrews were in control of Shechem throughout the time their brethren were in Egyptian bondage."

He continued: "So the sojourn in and Exodus from Egypt, and the desert wanderings that followed, involved only part of the Israelite nation."14 The Bible clearly states that all of the family of Jacob migrated into Egypt. However, Johnson agrees with the idea that the Exodus "occurred towards the last quarter of the second millennium B.C... in the reign of the famous Rameses II (1304-1237 B.C.)."15

But, simultaneously, Johnson appears to have contradicted himself when he wrote: "But it is not probable that the exodus itself took place in Rameses' reign. It seems more likely that the Israelites broke out under his successor: Merneptah."16 He then suggested that the Exodus occurred in stages, not in one bold exit.17 And, he added:

> Something happened at the frontiers of Egypt, that persuaded the eyewitnesses that God had intervened directly and decisively in their fate. The way it was related and set down convinced subsequent generations that this unique demonstration of God's mightiness on their behalf was the most remarkable event in the whole history of nations.18

In this argument, Johnson's tone suggests that he doubted the biblical record, which is, that the Exodus was an act of God. But he does point to the military obstacle to Israel's escape by night. He wrote: "What we do know is that the frontier was heavily defended in places and policed throughout. ...19 He paid tribute to the towering centrality of Moses in the Exodus narrative.

According to Johnson, "Moses is the fulcrum-figure in Jewish history, the hinge around which it all turns."20 He challenged the views of those who think that "Moses was a later fiction and the Mosaic code a fabrication of the post-Exilic priests in the second half of the first millennium B.C."21

He insisted that "Moses was beyond the power of the human mind to invent, and his power leaps out from the page of the Bible narrative, as it once imposed itself on a difficult and divided people, often little better than a frightened mob."22

Moses was not a superman, "a superhuman one." He was a man with human weaknesses and failings. See these in his irate temperament and family life. But, he was still one of the "archetypes of men whose strengths and achievements were to illuminate Jewish history again and again,"23 men like Joseph, Abel, Isaac, Jacob, David and

Solomon. The Bible says that "Moses was very meek (gentle, kind, and humble) ... above all the men on the face of the earth" (Numb. 12:3).

Johnson summarized Moses' attributes as follows: "Above all, he was a lawmaker and judge, the engineer of a mighty framework to enclose in a structure of rectitude every aspect of public and private conduct – a totalitarian of the spirit."24

Abraham, Isaac and Jacob may have been the Jewish patriarchs, but "Moses was the essentially creative force, the moulder of the people; under him and through him, they became a distinctive people, with a future as a nation."25 Africa needs many men and women like Moses, the Jewish revolutionary. See what an edifice and legacy he had left behind him!

I agree that Moses could not have been the product of any man's intellectual fabrications. He was, as the Bible frequently tells us, "the man of God" (Ps. 90:1). He was truly the leader of the Jewish people. There has been none like him ever since (except for Elijah) until the advent of Jesus Christ.

Howard Fast, another biographer of the Jewish people, in his book, The Jews: Story of a People (1968), claimed that his book was the history of a monotheistic concept and a nonviolent ethic. He wrote that the book was about a people who worshipped the God of Moses and built an empire in the days of King David and Solomon, his son. This book was republished in 2006.

We still may ask: "What was the origin of the Jews? If ever they were slaves in Egypt, how did their emancipation occur?" Unfortunately, Howard Fast provides us with scanty information on these matters. His responses cover only six pages within his 338-page book. But he is very emphatic about the personality and role of Moses in Jewish history.

Fast insists that Moses' name was Egyptian, African, not Jewish. He wrote that Moses' name means "a child is given."26 Moses once married an African woman and I believe that African scholars ought to trace the roots of that marriage to discover the African line of his ancestry. We may benefit from this research as we will discover more of the African connection with Israel.

Few scholars, Fast declared, have questioned the fact that Moses' name is African, Egyptian. Then, he adds:

Without Moses, the Jews are unthinkable, unimaginable, and here I talk of Jews specifically, in both the historical and contemporary sense. ... Moses was the Jew. He stepped into history as the Jew, and so the Jew stepped into history, and became so much a part of it.27

In other words, there would have been no Jewishness without Moses. He is the bearer of their identity. One may say the same thing about the Jewish religion – Judaism, which was founded upon the Decalogue by Moses and the Pentateuch, the first five books of the Old Testament.

Regarding the Exodus (the Revolution), Fast had this to say:

We know only this, that sometime in the thirteenth century before our era, probably during the long reign of Ramses II, a man called Moses led his followers out of Egypt. ... Ramses II [was] the Pharaoh of the exodus ... We are fairly certain the king who enslaved them was Ramses II.28

So, Howard Fast agrees with the date of 1250 B. C. as the year Ramses II enslaved the Hebrews,29 but he disagrees with the number of people who left Egypt. He writes that "No more than a thousand of them and most likely only five or six hundred. He accomplished the manumission not by violence but by the force of his personality."30

That "force of his personality," I contend, was from Yahweh, the God of Moses. That was what brought about the nonviolent revolution for the ancient Hebrews. The Bible commentator, Finis Jennings Dake, reminds us that "Moses was in supernatural business,"31 performing 42 miracles, beginning with his call in Midia.

In the 10 plagues which afflicted Egypt, 54 acts of God were displayed. The plagues, Dake wrote, were aimed at delivering Israel and preparing Aaron and Moses for such divine deliverance (Ex. 3: 17-22; 4: 21-23; and 8: 13).32 If any of Moses' words, miracles and predictions had failed, it would have portrayed God as being a liar. The plagues and miracles were meant to show Pharaoh that Yahweh was greater than all the gods of Egypt.

Moreover, no earthly man or god could withstand the great power of Almighty God. The death of Pharaoh's firstborn son, the likely heir to the Egyptian throne, was particularly instructive. God had the power to slay anyone who worked against His will and would not tolerate any opposition.

The theologian, Walter C. Kaiser, Jr., asserted that "the plagues had a salvific purpose for both Israel and Egypt. They were to convince Pharaoh that Yahweh indeed had spoken and had to be feared and obeyed; Israel had no choice and neither did the Egyptians."33 Thus, the revolution was God's unique deliverance without human effort (Ex. 3: 8 and 6: 6-7).

The miracles which were wrought by Moses authenticated his power (Ex. 4: 20-21), even to call upon his God to split the waters of the Red Sea. And, why is it incredible to human minds that the great and Almighty God was capable of performing such a feat? The ten plagues effected Israel's release while the miraculous signs guided the people's path as they headed for the Promised Land.

Another Old Testament theologian and author, Paul R. House admonished that "the supernatural viewpoint in Exodus should not necessarily disqualify the accounts as nonhistorical ... It is not fair to eliminate Exodus's historicity on [the] grounds" of its supernaturalness. ... Professor House points out that the Passover came to be observed "as a day that mark[ed] a particular point when Israel was delivered from Egypt."34

G. E. Wright, another Christian author, while pointing out that Israel was known to the Egyptians about 1220 B.C., emphasized the historical significance of the Exodus through the Passover festival and the Feast of the Tabernacles, the former held in the spring of the year and the later in the Fall.

It is to be remembered that between 457 B.C. and 432 B. C., both Ezra and Nehemiah revived these celebrations, showing how central and important these were to their faith and worship. They were NOT celebrating a myth. But, the Exodus gave rise to a language which embodied such words and phrases like "deliver," "redeem," "salvation," "bring out," "mighty acts," and "lead forth." These terms are central to biblical soteriology.

The Exodus aided Israel's understanding of God's righteousness and their conception of themselves as His chosen people or "the Elect" of God. Henceforth, they could count upon their God as <u>their</u> Redeemer, Savior, and Deliverer. They could call on Him in times of national crises and they often did.

It is obvious that the causes of the Hebrew revolution were slavery and tyranny by the ruling class in Egypt. Additionally, the arrogance and stubbornness of Pharaoh was another cause. The Bible tells us that God had heard the cries of the Israelites and seen the oppression of His people. He also had seen the exploitation of His people. The result was God's miraculous intervention, since the Israelites could <u>never</u> have freed themselves.

The Egyptians lost their slaves and their slave labor. According to the Bible, Pharaoh lost part of his military establishment. The nation-state of Israel was born. There was also a new birth of freedom and liberty. Israel was to celebrate this year of liberty. This new nation became God's sign-post to the world. It has been so and much more since 1948 when the modern state of Israel was reborn. This was also another miracle.

Africans can draw lessons from these historical events. The first lesson is that there is a God in this universe. This God is not dead but very much alive and well. He can act on the behalf of those who love and trust Him. He is the Savior, Redeemer and Deliverer of the nations that acknowledge Him. He is powerful and Almighty.

The second lesson from the Hebrew Revolution we can learn is that God will not forever tolerate the oppression and exploitation of the weak and the poor. He will come sooner than one may think to their rescue and can come suddenly. God is compassionate to them, too.

God is able to sustain the individuals and nations that look to Him. Africans have a promise in Psalm 68: 31, "Princes shall come from Egypt; Ethiopia shall stretch forth her hands unto God." Many people who understand the working of God on earth believe that decolonization, the rise of the African nations in the last century, and the emergence of Barack Obama in the first decade of the 21st century is a sign that the Davidic prophecy is about to be completely fulfilled with regards to Africa.

Africans must be assured that God will answer when they whole-heartedly call out to Him. The faith of the Africans in God has a historical foundation in the God of the Israelites who is also the God of the whole Earth (Is. 45: 22).

As a people, who had been enslaved and colonized for over 500 years, our God is not deaf if we earnestly cry out to Him as the ancient Hebrews did before Moses emerged. Atheists may mock as they will at this thought. But God shall laugh at their derision. We, Africans, can safely say: "Tyrants, BEWARE. There is a God in heaven!"

THE ENGLISH "GLORIOUS" REVOLUTION

The English people of the United Kingdom have fought many wars, including the War of the Roses (1455-1485). But they have had only one war which they refer to as the "Glorious Revolution" (1688-1689). The history of the English dates back to 55 B.C., if one goes by the exaggerated narrative by Winston Churchill, their former Prime Minister and World War II hero.

One can also say that the history of the English people goes only as far back as 1707, when the Act of Union was established.35 It was this Act which joined England with Scotland to produce Great Britain. Today, Britain or the United Kingdom is essentially an island country of 94, 248 square miles, 300 miles wide and 600 miles long. It is made up of the political units of Scotland, England, Wales and northern Ireland.

The English people were not always Christians. They were initially heathens and pagans. According to F. F. Bruce, the Church historian and author, "the earliest date in the history of British Christianity is August 1, 314 A.D."36 The lasting legacy of the English people to the world is their language, which has become the <u>lingua franca</u> of the international community. As we shall soon see, the "Glorious Revolution" has had a global impact upon modern man.

This revolution occurred within the era in European history known as "The Age of Absolutism" dated from 1660 to 1789. Absolutism has been defined as "the conscious extension of the legal and administrative power of state sovereigns over their subjects, and over the vested interests of the social and economic orders in which those subjects were ranked."37

This Euro-centric idea of politics and governance had manifested itself in England as far back as the 16th century. Simply stated, absolutism was the tyrannical, despotic, or dictatorial form of government by which a monarch ruled and reigned by a divine right which he believed he had the power to do. When such a monarch exceeded his powers as allowed by Parliament and his subjects, he was in deep trouble.

Particularly in the years from 1789 to 1848, a period Eric

Hobsbawm calls "the Age of Revolution,"38 a monarch could face rebellion, anarchy or even deposition. Between 1642 and 1649, King Charles I of England faced such a crisis which led to a Civil War and, eventually, his execution. The so-called "Glorious Revolution" came 39 years later.

There were important antecedents to this revolution. One was the Magna Carta (or the Great Charter) of 1215. There were many civil wars in England but the king was never executed in any of them. But the most significant was that in which the king was tried and hanged in 1649.

From 1649 to 1658, England was ruled by a despot known to us as Oliver Cromwell. After Cromwell, Charles II was "restored" to the monarchy and he ruled for 25 years, (1660-1685). He was followed by James II who ruled England for only three years, from 1685 to 1688.

Historians tell us that prior to 1215, the time was characterized by global upheavals.39 In his book, <u>A Constitutional and Legal History of England</u> (1990), author Goldwin Smith describes that era as "years of danger,"40 and adds :

> When Stephen died in 1154 England was full of anarchy and anarchy nourishes nothing. When Henry II died in 1189 a profound revolution had taken place. Fertility had been the constant note of his rule. He had brought order. He had temporarily tamed the great feudatories. He had plucked the flower safely from the nettle danger. And soon the prospect was altered again.41

What was "altered again" was the order, peace and stability which Henry II had introduced. Historian Asa Briggs described those years of English feudalism as exploitative. While a monarch's wealth and power increased and widened, the ordinary English people were increasingly poor and poorer. They were burdened with many cares and concerns, including heavy and vexing taxes.

The general attitude toward the poor was reflected in this quote from a 12th century theologian: "Servitude is ordained by God, either because of the sins of those who become serfs, or as a trial, in order that those who are thus humbled may be made better."42 In a word, the English Church justified exploitation and oppression of the poor!

The English society was stratified with the king, his nobles and lords, at the top, followed by the barons, middle-class professionals, traders, peasants and slaves at the bottom, in that order. England was not greatly endowed with natural and mineral resources. This is one reason she had to traverse over land and sea in search of wealth.

And, she used every cruel and diabolical means, including trafficking in human beings, piracy and robbery, to get rich and wealthy. Nearly everyone depended upon the land. The tiny island, which called herself "Great," had been conquered by the Romans in 43 A.D. and later by the Normans in 1066 A.D.43 Again, Briggs wrote that "there was a continual threat from the sea as well as from the land," and "the coastline was always vulnerable to attack."44

"English land had to be worked in English weather. It was farmed laboriously and passed down from one generation to another through different inheritance customs."45 The people were either free or unfree, depending upon a mindset that held that all men and women were either rich or poor.

Christianity "did nothing to change the basic economics"46 of the English people. So, the <u>Magna Carta</u> came in 1215 to address some socio-political and economic inequalities. The Charter was drafted in a hurry. Briggs noted that "it was largely because of disputes about taxation – pressure on the pocket is more quickly felt than pressure on the mind – that [King] John was forced by his barons to seal the Magna Carta in 1215."47

Military expenses from many of the king's wars had irritated many of King John's most powerful subjects. So, the Magna Carta "dealt essentially with privileges claimed by Norman barons," and "it was to become part of the English constitutional inheritance because claims for privileges set out in its clauses could in time be translated into the universal language of freedom and justice."48

Scholars today who have re-examined the subject of the Great Charter say that the document has become the root of modern freedom.49 But, we must understand that neither the efforts of Henry II nor the provisions of the Magna Carta, were able to make the English a peace-loving people.

The fundamental problems of taxation without representation, Church and State conflicts, and general economic matters continued. The intolerable arrogance of the monarchy could not be curtailed. The result of these circumstances was constant war and chaos within the English nation.

Charles I was born into this world of circumstances. He was the second son of James VI of Scotland (later James I of England). He was born in Dunfermline, Scotland, on November 19, 1600. In his youth, he was a stutterer and had a moral weakness in lying. However, he had a good education. In 1623, he traveled to Spain in the hope of marrying a woman there; but he failed after five months because the Spanish king at the time considered him a heretic.

He returned to England to instigate war against Spain but, at the same time, sought to marry a French princess, Henrietta Maria, sister of King Louis VIII. He thought that his plans would secure an alliance with France against Spain. On March 27, 1625, he was crowned King of England, at the age of 25.

On May 1, 1625, his marriage with Henrietta was secured in France by proxy. However, many Protestants in England did not like having a Catholic Queen on the throne. And, to make matters worse, the French did not believe that Charles I was faithful in the marriage. The English, on the other hand, did not believe that the French were active enough in their current war against Spain. In 1627, Charles foolishly declared war against the French while also engaging in war with Spain. It was a no-win situation.

These wars caused Parliament to meet frequently because money had to be provided to support the War efforts. Also, there were differences between Parliament and Charles I over war supplies, religion, and economic policies. These differences were summed up in a document known as the Petition of Right of 1628. It stated the grievances which the English people had against their king.

King Charles's arbitrary taxation policy and imprisonments were roundly condemned by the House of Commons. But, the primary cause of the king's problems was the resentment the English aristocracy had over the continued ascendancy of the Duke of Buckingham.

Also, King Charles was discredited in the eyes of the aristocracy over the failed policies of the Duke against Spain in 1625 and the disastrous attack against the French in 1627. Did no one ever tell the English that their king was but a youth – he was only 25!

When the Duke of Buckingham was assassinated in 1628, loyalty to the king was divided. Discontentment was widespread. Although the wars against Spain and France were stopped, Charles I was preoccupied with hunting and collecting immense artwork from all over Europe, while England suffered. He grew increasingly in love with Henrietta Maria.

In 1640, Parliament was summoned to meet again in order to respond to the enforcement of order in the English Church, an order which had been extended to Scotland in 1637. This was another cause for resentment against the king. In 1641, the king was forced to relinquish many of his ministers and to agree to some reforms. He did not like that.

Therefore, on January 4, 1642, Charles I appeared before Parliament with some soldiers, in an attempt to arrest five of the leaders who opposed him. These were charged with treason. But Charles failed in his attempt. Then, he called upon all his loyal subjects to defend his divine right to rule as he deemed fit. It was at this stage that a civil war began.50

Oliver Cromwell (already mentioned), Henry Ireton, Thomas Fairfax, and John Milton (the famous English poet) constituted the opposition to Charles. Others were members of Parliament known as the Roundheads, the House of Commons (usually the Puritans), merchants and naval officers. Charles I was supported by the Royalists (known as the Cavaliers, including the Roman Catholics), members of the Church of England, and the House of Lords.

Each side raised an army of about 70,000 men. In the war that ensued, Charles I was defeated. Simon Schama, an author on British history, claims that a greater proportion of the English population died during their Civil War than did in the First World War.

There was no legal method in England at the time to try a king for high treason (waging war against the fatherland). So, a new Court of Justice was hastily constituted and was led by Ireton. The trial lawyer was John Cooke. Charles I refused to recognize the authority of the new court. But, on June 30, 1649, he was convicted, condemned and executed.

Diane Purkiss, another English authority on the Civil War, concluded that the war was a struggle between the monarchy and Parliament. She believed that the struggle concerned fundamental questions of sovereignty and political rights. The war dealt with the obstinacy of the monarchy, the rejection of the divine right to rule, and a change of course in the way that Western governments perceive politics.

Another revolution was in the way but at a price. That price was regicide (the murdering of a king). The brutal persecution of Royalists and of English Catholics came to an end.51 One of the tragedies of the English political system was the continued dominance and oppression by the monarchy against the ordinary people.

For example, even after Charles II was "restored," John Cooke was brutally executed at the hands of Charles II as a revenge for his father. Cooke sacrificed his life to make tyranny a crime.52 The historian Mark Kishlansky summarized the brutalities and counter-brutalities of that era when he wrote as follows:

> The savagery felt by those royalists aching for revenge was done to the corpses of Cromwell, Ireton, and Bradshaw, which were disinterred, dismembered and disgraced. Cromwell's head set on a pole outside Westminster Hall, was on view for a quarter-century. ... There were eleven public executions. ...53

By 1688, the English people had had enough of tyranny and bloodshed. The War of the Roses (1455-1485), the 30 Years' War (1618-1648), and the Anglo-Spanish War (1655-1660) had exhausted the country. Moreover, the three Dutch Wars (1660-1665; 1665-1667; and 1674-1678) were too recent in the minds of the English people for any engagement in another conflict. Add to all these the 100 Years War which began in 1337 and had also tired out the people.54

Unfortunately, for the English people, Charles II (1660-1685), who was "restored" to the monarchy, turned out not to have learned any lessons from his father. He was young and wanted to continue the divine right of kingship. He did not accept the limitations on the powers of the monarchy.

Moreover, James II (1685-1689) was weakened by an imminent attack from William of Orange in 1688. When he crossed the English Channel into England, William's "conquest" was without blood since Charles II had fled the country, allowing Parliament to declare the throne vacant. For the English, then, this "revolution" without a war was, indeed, "glorious."55 William and Mary became the new sovereigns over England.

More significantly, a new Bill of Rights, passed by Parliament, was accepted by the new monarchs. This Bill reaffirmed the English civil liberties such as trial by jury, habeas corpus (guarantee of a speedy trial for an accused person), right of petition and redress, and the requirement that the monarch be under the laws of the land.

In 1689, an Act of Toleration granted dissenters the right to worship, though not the right to full political protection. And, toleration was by no means a guarantee of religious freedom as we know it today. But England was on her way to the establishment of both political and religious freedoms, precedents unheard-of in world history up until that time.

In his book, <u>Our First Revolution</u> (2007), Michael Barone stated that the "Glorious Revolution" led to representative governments and the guarantee of liberties enjoyed by many people today. Furthermore, Barone argued that this revolution laid the foundations for global capitalism. It also led to the adoption of a foreign policy which can aggressively oppose foreign powers.

Barone believed that the revolution of 1688 sprang from the character of the English people. He wrote that the Glorious Revolution depended upon the talents, audacity and good luck of William of Orange (later to become William III of England) and John Churchill, the ancestor of Winston Churchill. Without the success of the 1688 revolution, Barone insisted, the American Revolution of 1776 may never have occurred. In other words, the Glorious Revolution had global implications.56

However, some scholars write that "1688 was not all glory," and that it actually consolidated the wealth of the already rich landowners. It restored the status quo in preference for the "wealthy social and economic order."57 It brought nothing but misery to the English Catholics who were disenfranchised, particularly in Scotland. But it did bring an end to absolutism.

The relevance of this study of the English "Glorious" Revolution to the African political situation cannot be over-emphasized. First, it should not be forgotten that, for much of Africa, England was their colonial master. Colonialism, by its very nature, brought to Africa a culture of absolutism which plagued and continues to plague Africa for 50 years after her independence. England is responsible for much of the MESS in Africa today.

Africans can learn a lot from this study, just as the American

Founding Fathers did. The African masses can take courage in the belief that the despots, tyrants and dictators among them will one day flee, just as Charles II fled to France to stay there permanently.

Idi Amin and Mariam Mengistu are examples of this hope. They are no more in power. But if these tyrants would not flee, then Africans must commit what would be tantamount to regicide in each of the 53 countries which make up Africa, so that the motherland can have her Glorious Revolution. This will be Africa's blessed hope and a signal to a wonderful era for all of us who love Africa.

THE AMERICAN REVOLUTION

On July 4, 1776, Britain lost all of her 13 colonies in North America. The sun had began to set on England. Those colonies formally declared their independence, severed their allegiance and loyalty to Britain. The loss was not without a bloody fight which lasted for seven years. What led to this state of affairs and what can Africans learn from it?

The answer to the first part of the question goes far back to 1763 when England concluded a treaty with France in order to end the Seven Years' War (1756-1763). George III had become the king of England in 1760. Britain had successfully ousted France from North America. The victory over France cost England a heavy war debt.

Consequently, the English Parliament imposed revenue raising taxes for the first time upon the colonies, in addition to the customs' duties which had long regulated trade. The colonies resisted the new taxes and tensions arose and increased. From 1764 to 1770, no less than five new tax measures were introduced. These taxes were:

1. the Sugar Act, 1764
2. the Currency Act, 1764
3. the Stamp Act, 1765 (repealed in 1766)
4. the Declaratory Act, 1766
5. the Townshend Acts, 1767, and repealed in 1770.

The Tea tax (1773) was one of the Townshend Acts still in effect and was designed to save the East India Company from bankruptcy. But it presumably caused the Boston Tea Party and the so-called "Boston Massacre" in which only five people were killed.

In 1774, some new laws, known collectively as the Coercive and Quebec Acts, were introduced to punish Bostonians and the colony of Massachusetts for the Tea Party. In fairness to the colonies, it seemed that the British Parliament was harassing and provoking the colonies by the sheer force and number of the Acts.58

Some twenty years earlier, a 22-year-old young man named George Washington, then a colonel, had fought in the Seven Years' War on the British side. He was defeated by the French at Fort Necessity, near Great Meadows, Pennsylvania. That was on July 3, 1754. He had surrendered and the French allowed him and his soldiers to return to Virginia.59

How was it, then, that 20 years later, the same Washington was opposed to the British, perhaps reluctantly, now allied with his former enemies, the French, and was headed to become the Father of the new Republic of the United States of America? We should also ask, how "revolutionary" was the American Revolution?60 Were the Americans justified in rebelling against Britain and her Parliament?

To the first question, we respond that between 1754 and April 19, 1775, when war broke out, a revolution was brewing and growing in intensity in those 21 years. A person can analyze one of those Acts to discover three aspects of it that were displeasing to the Americans. First, the taxes were levied on items coming in from Britain, not from other countries. To the Americans, the taxes were at odds with the mercantilist theory of the time.

Second, those taxes raised money for the salaries of certain royal officials in the colonies. This posed a direct challenge to the authority of the colonial assemblies. Thirdly, the Townshend Acts aimed to create an American Board of Customs Commissioners and of the Vice-Admiralty courts in Boston, Philadelphia and Charleston, South Carolina. Merchants were angry because their profits were likely to be threatened.

In addition, Charles Townshend had proposed the appointment of a Secretary of State for American Affairs and the suspension of the New York Legislature for refusing to comply with the Quartering Act of 1765. The Act required that colonial governments supply certain items like firewood and candles to British troops permanently stationed in America.61

What emerges from the implementation of the British imposed taxes was that **the British policy makers did not handle the colonies well**

as British subjects who deserved fairness and equality under the principles of good governance which every Englishman deserved to enjoy. The colonists felt they were slighted and not sufficiently consulted before the Acts were promulgated and executed.

It is true, however, that the war debt incurred by Britain, had doubled between 1754 and 1776. In 1754, the debt was 73 million pounds. By 1776, it had risen to 137 million pounds! The English people themselves were already heavily taxed. Therefore, in the opinion of this writer, it seemed quite natural, fair and justified that the colonists shared in bearing the burden of the national debt. After all, the colonists considered themselves to be English citizens. They were not yet Americans.

British power in North America had benefited the colonists and protected them from the Indians, the French and the Spanish from 1607, when Virginia was occupied, and from 1620, when Plymouth, Massachusetts, was founded. The demand to share in the war debts was a little price for the blessings of being Englishmen and women. The rejection of the Acts was based on colonial self-interest and selfishness, to say the least.

How "revolutionary" was the American Revolution? To answer this question, we turn to M. Stanton Evans who, in his book, <u>The Theme is Freedom</u> (1994), stated that "The American Revolution was hostile to any and all ideas of unfettered power. ... This was indeed the very essence of the struggle."62 This statement reminds us of the results of the English "Glorious" Revolution of 1688.

Evans added: "The constant theme of the colonials was that they were loyal true-blue Englishmen, devoted to the British constitution and hence to British freedoms."63 If so, then, why did they resist the Acts and the war debt? Evans went on to state that "the colonists had a high regard for England and its tradition, and constantly made their plea for liberty in this spirit."64

The colonists, Evans argued, wanted all "the rights of free-born Englishmen."65 <u>Ipso facto</u>, those colonists ought to have shared in the costs and privileges of maintaining and enjoying the freedoms allowed under the banner of the English flag. Rebellion was mischievous and unpatriotic. It was treasonable and George Washington knew that very well. So, what really instigated the rebellion?

The <u>methods</u> adopted by the British and her Parliament were arbitrary, seemingly unfair, and signaled the high-handedness of the monarchy, even of George III and his administrators. Those administrators did not seem to understand that the colonies had matured and were already enjoying some degrees of independence by virtue of their long distance location from England. It had been 169 years since the colonists first arrived in Virginia!

England ought to have understood that the conditions of life in the New World were different. The colonists constantly faced the threats of annihilation from their neighbors: the Indians, the French and the Spanish. Thus, they needed to be handled differently than the people back home in England. But, this is not to say that the colonists were totally excused from their responsibilities since they were Englishmen and nothing else. Their racial and national identity at the time was English.

The popular view today is that the Americans were fighting for freedom. Nothing could be farther from the truth. To be truthful, <u>the colonists were never slaves in need of freedom!</u> The white colonists were not fighting for freedom; they were fighting for justice, fairness and equality, to be treated as fellow Englishmen and women.

In actuality, the white colonists held a segment of their population – the African Americans – in chattel slavery from 1619 to 1865 (a period of 246 years). The slaves were the ones who desperately needed freedom. White Americans were at the time already free. Therefore, the clamor for freedom was an afterthought, a red-herring and a propaganda for war.

The propagandists were men like Patrick Henry, of "Give Me Liberty or Give Me Death" fame; Thomas Paine who was made famous by his published pamphlet, <u>Common Sense</u>, and Benjamin Franklin, now regarded as the "the oldest revolutionary."66 There were many others, but the decision to go to war against their fellow Englishmen was neither a unanimous decision among the colonial leaders nor was it easy.

There were Loyalists and Patriots, supporters of the king and of the colonies, respectively. A Loyalist often faced the threat of death from a lynch mob, arson, banishment, extra taxes, and property confiscation. At the same time, the Indians were ready to take the opportunity to revolt. The slaves were caught up in a dilemma. Certainly, there was no consensus on the matter of "freedom."

John Mein, a Bostonian bookseller and newspaper publisher, had to flee to England and never returned again to Boston.67 A woman named Betsy Cumming fled into Nova Scotia because she opposed the war for independence. Many other people were persecuted and their properties burned down, confiscated, or looted because they dared to oppose the war.

In Philadelphia, "resistance leaders were dismayed when an angry mob threatened to attack Benjamin Franklin's house."68 The radicals and conservatives fought each other openly. Loyalists and neutrals were rarely tolerated as they were deemed to be saboteurs or betrayers of the colonial cause.69 At last, victory came in 1782 with great assistance from the French.70

This victory achieved the following <u>six</u> things:

1. unconditional independence for Americans
2. new boundaries for the United States were fixed (I should add that later, American expansionism breached this agreement)
3. Florida was returned to Spain
4. a ragtag army had taken on the greatest military power in the world at the time and won
5. Americans gave up their British identity forever
6. a republican government was established, instead of a monarchy.71

The newly won "freedom" was for the propertied class of white adult males. They only could vote and be voted for. Women, even white women, could not vote nor be voted for until 1920's, more than 200 years later! African Americans were not beneficiaries of the new freedom. They remained in bondage until 1865 after another revolution – the Civil War in which 620,000 lives perished – was waged and won. Four million slaves received their freedom at last.

Now, had King George III and his Parliament <u>wisely</u> settled their differences with the colonists, one wonders if there would have been <u>any</u> talk of revolution or freedom.72 In my opinion, the American war for independence was the price paid for the British lack of wisdom and diplomacy, their intransigence and arbitrariness in dealing with political and economic problems.73

Granted that there was an American revolution, what really was the meaning of the Revolution so that the African people might learn something from it? Luckily for us, we have many interpreters of that event. We begin with the opinion of John Adams (1735-1826). He was the second U.S. President, after George Washington.

In a letter dated February 13, 1818, which President Adams sent to Hezekiah Niles (1777-1839), who was the editor of the <u>Weekly Register</u>, Adams explained that "the real American Revolution" was "the radical change in the principles, opinions, sentiments, and affections" which the people of America held toward the British.74

According to Adams, the war for independence was <u>not</u> the Revolution since "the Revolution was effected before the war commenced." "The Revolution," Adams wrote, "was in the minds and hearts of the people; a change in their religious sentiments of their duties and obligations."75

The Revolution began when Americans felt that King George III was "bent upon the destruction of all the securities of their lives, liberties, and properties, they thought it their duty" not to reserve allegiance for England but "to pray for the continental congress and all the thirteen congresses. ..."

Also, the Revolution began as the protection provided by Britain in the past was withdrawn and the Americans "thought allegiance was dissolved." The Revolution began when Americans "found [Britain] a cruel beldam, willing like Lady Macbeth, to 'dash their brains out,' it was no wonder if their filial affections ceased, and were changed into indignation and horror."76

Adams added that there was a "great and important alteration in the religious, moral, political, and social character of the people of the thirteen colonies," even though the colonies were "all distinct, unconnected, and independent of each other." He wrote about the need for the generations after his own to do more research into the matter of their revolutionary origins.

Americans were to search and collect "all the records, pamphlets, newspapers, and even handbills, which in any way contributed to change the temper and views of the people, and compose them into an independent nation."77 Such research was meant to discover how the colonies found unity in their diversity. It was also meant to recognize the global impact of the revolution in South America and in all other countries.

Adams believed that such studies would reveal some lessons from the Revolution, namely,

> they may teach mankind that revolutions are no trifles; that they ought never to be undertaken rashly; nor without deliberate consideration and sober reflection; nor without a solid, immutable, eternal foundation of justice and humanity; nor without a people possessed of intelligence, fortitude, and integrity sufficient to carry them with steadiness, patience, and perseverance, through all the vicissitudes of fortune, the trials and melancholy disasters they may have to encounter.78

No one could have said it better than this eyewitness to history. For, in the above paragraph, Adams laid down for all time the recipe and requisites for any revolutionary action anywhere in the world. His words re-echoed those of Chairman Mao when he said that a revolution is not a dinner party. At least here, the Founding Fathers seem to have understood what they were about.

Adams recommended an annual celebration of July 4, 1776, "in commemoration of the principles and feelings which contributed to produce the revolution."79 The rest of his letter to Niles dealt with the history of the time, from 1760 to 1776 and thereafter, biographical sketches of his colleagues such as James Otis, Samuel Adams, John Hancock, and many others, and their English backgrounds.

Historians like Edmund S. Morgan, Bernard Bailyn, and Gordon S. Wood have fulfilled Adams's wishes and predictions. Their work is known to students of American intellectual thought. For example, Morgan, Bailyn and Wood have shown that there were ideological origins of the American Revolution. Wood, in particular, points out that the American Revolution meant disaster for native American Indians who were nearly annihilated by Christian white Americans.

About half a million Loyalists were forced to leave the United States but the Revolution imbued upon Americans a deep obsession for education, especially the brand of education known as pragmatism.80 The Revolution's dreams and ideals were fully expressed in the national Constitution that was crafted.

Charles A. Beard was also a historian who believed that the meaning of the Revolution lay in understanding the economic motives of the Founding Fathers. Thus, author Edward Countryman, confirming

Beard's position, wrote that "the Revolution's victors wanted land."81 As soon as victory was in sight, New Englanders moved West, to occupy new territory.

Also, Countryman believed that liberty was at the center of the Revolution but he added that there were equally class interests.82 While Beard held that the U. S. Constitution was "an economic document,"83 Countryman believed that a deep distrust of power and of government was part of the origins of the Revolution.

In his 308-page book, Dan Mabry Lacy included a chapter which he titled, "The Meaning of the American Revolution."84 Lacy argued that the great lesson of the American Revolution was that a nation can emerge shaped by an idea – the idea that all men are created equal. A nation can be "conceived in liberty."85

Lacy believed that there were <u>four</u> important developments at the time of the American Revolution, namely, secession, the development of a political theory or philosophy, the Constitution, and democracy for the new nation. But, said Lacy, the meaning of the revolution could not be found in any one of those developments but in <u>all</u> of them.

"The political idea of the Revolutionary thinkers cannot be fully understood apart from their economic ideas and from the nature of the American economy of the time."86 Then Lacy added: "The meaning of the American Revolution for other countries and for subsequent generations is to be found not in the words uttered in 1776 but in the survival of its principles in the living institutions of other lands and later times."87

In other words, America held out and continues to hold out a conceived dream for mankind's victory over anarchy and tyranny. And, it was to this dream that Martin Luther King, Jr., appealed in many of his great orations during the Civil Rights Movement, which is considered by some to be the third American Revolution.

In his own edited work, <u>The Meaning of the American Revolution</u> (1969), Lawrence H. Leder cited the historian, Henry Steele Commager as saying that the significance of the American Revolution today lies in our understanding of what truly happened in 1776. Commager said:

> If we hope to understand what went on in this country in the last third of the eighteenth century, ... We must recognize the distinction between the American Revolution and the War for Independence. ... The War for Independence was merely a part

of [the] larger movement … the Revolution was a constructive rather than a destructive period. It is not the disruption of one empire that is important; it is the success of Americans in finding solutions to [their] problems.88

Commager highlighted six factors which inspired the Revolution: the tyranny of King George III of England, royal despotism, discontentment, sectional and class divisions in the colonies, religious and political dissenters, and free-land seekers.

He concluded that the war galvanized or brought together all the sectional and divisive interests, especially as the war was "fought on the theory that men are equal, that men make governments, and that government derives authority from the consent of the governed."89

The Revolutionary Founders were architects "of a new social and economic order."90 Commager noted that, in keeping faith with the revolutionary ideals, land reforms followed the war's end. "The great estates of the Penns, the Fairfaxes, and the Granvilles were confiscated and sold to small farmers, while in New York millions of acres of loyalist estates were turned into farms for thousands of settlers."91

The demands of the underprivileged colonists were met. But in spite of all these positive measures from the Revolution, Commager hinted that a feeling of disappointment still persisted. The feeling was that "the Revolutionary Fathers were guilty of unseemly conduct … of short sightedness in surrendering the solid advantages of the British connection for the uncertain consequences of popular government."92

Yet, another view remains, which is, that the ideas which inspired the Revolution still survive through what is popularly known as the Jeffersonian democracy. In his essay, "Jefferson Still Lives," Saul K. Padover wrote that there is Jefferson the thinker, "the champion of the universal ideal of freedom, rather than … the American politician and statesman."93 This "thinking" Jefferson, Padover contended, is still popular in far away places like India, France, Asia and Africa.

Padover believed that "those interested in democracy as a political philosophy and system cannot ignore him,"94 referring to Jefferson, who is still very popular for his coherent political ideology, even though he owned slaves. Jefferson still stands tall for his ideas on human equality, freedom and the peoples' right to control their governments.

Padover observed that in 1789, the year that the French Revolution began, Jefferson penned the following words:

[T]here are rights which it is useless to surrender to the government, and which governments have yet always been found to invade. These are the rights of thinking, and publishing our thoughts by speaking or writing; the right of free commerce; the right of personal freedom.95

In a global context, herein lies the appeal of Thomas Jefferson and herein is the relevance of the American Revolution for our time, at least, in one sense. Hence, we can now answer our other question about the lessons which Africans can learn from the American Revolution.

First, it is imperative that Africans listen very carefully to the wise admonitions of the second U. S. President, John Adams. Revolutions, he said, are no trifles. They should never be undertaken rashly. They should never be undertaken without deliberate consideration and sober reflection.

Those half-wits and radicals in Africa who are contemplating a revolutionary action that has war and violence as their sole aim should read John Adams's letter again and again and ponder. They ought to bear in mind the words of Henry Steele Commager: a war for independence is NOT necessarily a revolution. Nor does it always yield the fruits of human freedom.

President Adams said that revolutionaries must be men and women possessed of intelligence, fortitude and integrity. I ought to add that they must have a vision, foresight and insight, bold, fearless and courageous; they must have commitment and convictions; they must have humility and, above all, wisdom and tact. They must know that real power belongs to God.96

I believe that it is time for the Africans to begin to ask some pertinent questions about the ideas and meaning of Africa, of an African renaissance, and of their destiny. The African thinkers must, like the early Americans, seek to know what ideas framed the coming of their respective Republics.

If there is to be a genuine African unity, it has to be grounded in the meeting of the minds of Africans and their ideas. We cannot simply be Africans solely because of our geographical identification or skin color! There must be some other concrete factors that bind us together so as to forge a common destiny.

But, above all, we must share in the American, and more so, human ideals of freedom, equality, and justice for all mankind. These, to me, constitute the ultimate reasons for an African World Revolution.

CHAPTER SEVEN
Learning From French, Russian & Chinese Revolutions

THE FRENCH REVOLUTION

In 1789, the American revolutionary leaders watched nervously and in horror as political events unfolded in France. They had cause to worry since one European out of every five lived in France.1 It had just been a little over a decade since their own declaration of independence from Britain. However, the French Revolution took place in stages: 1789-1792, 1792-1795, and 1799-1804.

Some scholars place the origin of the French people with the beginning of the Capetian dynasty in 987 A.D. But, many modern historians agree that the origins of the French people go back to Charles the Bald in 843 A.D. So, for about 203 years (1589-1792), the Capetian dynasty had an unbroken record of kingly rule over France. But, this record came to an end during the reign of Louis XVI on August 10, 1792. He had ruled for 18 years.

Louis XVI was born on August 23, 1754, in the city of Versailles. At an early age, he had a tendency to overeat and he loved hunting, science and geography. He married Marie Antoinette, the daughter of Emperor Francis I and Maria Theresa of Austria in 1770. He was only 16 at the time. He was crowned king on May 10, 1774 when he was only 20.

He was a devoted father and husband and was sincerely interested in the well-being of his people. However, Louis XVI had many weaknesses. He was indecisive and easily influenced by others. It should have been clear to the French king-makers that he was but a youth who lacked the ability to handle complex socio-political and economic national matters, like reforms and foreign policy.

At the beginning of his rule, Louis XVI restored the powers of the legislature to the Parlement (Parliament). But at the same time, he appointed A. R. Turgot as his First Minister in-charge- of reform matters, which was the main problem between the monarchy and the aristocracy.

Louis XVI had the virtues of an admirable private individual but did not possess enough of the leadership skills and vision to understand the revolutionary spirit of the time. This lack of vision contributed to the collapse of the monarchy and to his death. Like Charles I of England, Louis XVI was beheaded by his subjects on January 21, 1793, at the beginning of the second stage of the French Revolution.

Historians now say that the causes of the first stage of the Revolution which began in 1789 and ended a year before Louis XVI's execution were many and complex.2 The famous Edmund Burke, who was an eye-witness to the Revolution, blamed the French leadership for the conflict.

In his book, Reflections on the Revolution in France (1790), Burke stated as follows:

> France, by the perfidy of her leaders, has utterly disgraced the tone of lenient council in the cabinets of princes, and disarmed it of its most potent topics. She has sanctioned the dark suspicious maxims of tyrannous distrust; and taught kings to tremble at the delusive plausibilities of moral politicians.3

Burke was an Englishman who believed that "all circumstances taken together, the French revolution is the most astonishing that has hitherto happened in the world."4 He called Louis XVI "an arbitrary monarch" who "had the misfortune to be born king of France."5 However, Burke added that "misfortune is not crime," but that the government in France "was ... full of abuses."6

According to Burke, "the king of France [was] not the fountain of justice."7 Thus, Burke implied that the monarchy was responsible for some of the abuses within the realm. "In all other countries," Burke continued, "the office of ministers of state is of the highest dignity. In France it is full of peril and incapable of glory."8 In other words, the governmental machinery in France was corrupt.

Other notable critics and contemporaries of the time included Thomas Carlyle, the famed English essayist and William Wordsworth, the equally famous English romantic poet. Wordsworth was actually residing in Paris at the heyday of the Revolution.

These critics, along with the leaders of the Revolution, knew that what France needed most was "liberta."9 "Absolutism was the bane of continental noblemen."10 It is now agreed that there were, at least, <u>ten</u> factors which led to the French Revolution of 1789, namely:

1. tensions in the civil service (judiciary)
2. tensions among the clergy (Church)
3. tensions within the aristocracy (the military nobility)
4. political exclusivity
5. peasants who were overburdened
6. vestiges of the manorial system (land deprivations)
7. intellectual (role of ideas from such men like Thomas Paine)
8. the financial crisis (high prices of bread and inefficiency of the tax system)
9. personal character of the king (particularly his inability to control his wife)
10. the impact and success of the American Revolution.

By 1789, the French people were completely discontented. They had had it with the monarchy. They were ready to explode and, on July 14, a group of them stormed the Bastille where only seven prisoners were held. This storming of the Bastille was a symbol of their yearning for liberty and the fight against oppression for all the French citizens.

On that July 14, the leaders of the Revolution hoisted a new flag which signaled the birth of a new nation with the three ideals of liberty, equality and fraternity. Thus, the storming of the Bastille marked an end to the idea of an absolute monarch. Bastille Day became France's national holiday. Unlike the case in England regarding Charles I, the French revolutionaries did not commit regicide at this time.

But moderate reform measures were taken between 1789 and 1792. Also, the Revolutionary ideas penetrated into the hearts of the French people at this time. The destiny of France was in the hands of the members of the National Assembly.11

The ideological origins of the French Revolution hinged upon the fact that the Bastille "symbolized hated royal authority."12 When the crowds asked for arms from the officials in-charge of the prison, its governor "opened fire, killing ninety-eight"13 French citizens. The crowd then took revenge, captured the Bastille, and decapitated the governor.

Meanwhile, in the municipal areas, revolutionary governments were being set up throughout the country. The first stage of this Revolution was a time of "great fear," of peasant terrorism, especially when those peasants heard that the Revolution might not address their concerns.

Motivated by fear and uncertainty, peasants went wild committing widespread arson, destroying monasteries, residencies of bishops, and murdering some nobles who resisted. Women, also, angered by the high prices of bread and the rumors of Louis XVI's unwillingness to cooperate with their National Assembly, marched to Versailles on October 5, 1789, demanding to be heard.

The crowd broke through the palatial gates and demanded that their king return to Paris. The following day, their demand was met. The following were some of the <u>ten</u> successes of the first stage of the French Revolution:

1. manorialism was obliterated
2. the ecclesiastical tithes and corvee were abolished
3. hunting privileges of the nobles ceased
4. exemption from taxation and monopolies of all kinds stopped as these were considered contrary to natural equality
5. class and rank distinctions were removed and all French citizens were of equal status in the eyes of the law
6. the National Assembly prepared a charter of liberties. The result was the September 1789 "Declaration of the Rights of Man." Under this Declaration,
   (i)   property, liberty, and security and "resistance to oppression" were declared natural rights
   (ii) freedom of speech, religious toleration, and press freedom were declared inviolable

> (iii) all citizens were guaranteed equality of treatment in the courts
>
> (iv) no one was to be imprisoned or punished except in accordance with due process of law
>
> (v) sovereignty now resided in the people and civil servants were held liable for abuse of office and power.

7. In November 1789, the National Assembly decided to confiscate the lands of the Church. The following year in July, it passed a law – the Civil Constitution of the Clergy – which held that all bishops and priests be elected by the French people and be subject to State authority. The salaries of the clergy were also to be paid out of the public treasury. The clergy was to swear allegiance to the new law.

   This new rule was the beginning of the secularization of Christianity in France. The Roman Catholic Church in France had become oppressive and corrupt, earning the disdain and hatred of many French citizens. It had not been a truly national Church but one which owed her loyalty to the papacy in Rome.

8. In 1791, a new Constitution for France was drawn which:
   > (vi) provided a government with limited monarchy
   >
   > (vii) placed supreme power into the hands of the rich
   >
   > (viii) gave the franchise to those who paid a certain amount in taxes
   >
   > (ix) deprived the king of his control over the national army and local governments
   >
   > (x) disallowed the king's ministers membership in the National Assembly
   >
   > (xi) gave no power to the king over the legislature except the retainment of the veto.

9. The National Assembly could sell off Church lands to offset inflation and poverty. This action was expected to spur up economic growth.

10. Guilds and Trade Unions were abolished.

The "winners" at this stage of the Revolution were the upper middle-class.

The second stage of the French Revolution (1792-1795) marked the radical stage as Radical Republicans replaced the moderates. These radicals claimed to rule on the behalf of the common people. By the summer of 1792, disillusionment and disappointment by the common people had brought the downfall of the moderates.

One significant cause for the change was the lack of an effective national leader. King Louis XVI was grossly ineffective. Although the king was now 38 years old, he was dominated by his profligate wife. She cared for nothing else except her fashions and material things.

Moreover, the Queen did not care for the well-being of the French people but rather attracted their hatred. In particular, she was opposed to any national reforms. She was famous for her dictum: "Let them eat cake." Marie Antoinette encouraged the king to try to escape to Austria but the attempt failed.

The escape to Austria was aimed at rallying foreign military support for an attack against France. This was high treason and may have been one reason for the eventual execution of the king. After 1792, "France found itself at war with much of the rest of Europe."14

International support for the Revolution waned as there were many critics such as Edmund Burke, already cited. In Britain, anyone found in support of France and her Revolution was persecuted and punished. So much so was the opposition that anyone found with a copy of Thomas Paine's The Rights of Man (1791-1792) was imprisoned.

Austria and Prussia openly expressed deep concerns over the French Revolution. The two countries wanted a return to pre-revolutionary days. On April 20, 1792, the National Assembly of France declared war against Austria and Prussia. Immediately, almost all the political factions in France welcomed the decision to go to war.

Reactionaries, extremists and the Jacobins hoped to benefit from the war. The Jacobins believed in the universal suffrage which had not come to all French citizens. Jacobins were responsible for the national elections held in September 1792. The elections produced a governing body which ruled France for another three years, that is, from 1792 to 1795, the end of the second stage of the Revolution.

In the same election month, over 1,000 people were massacred as "enemies of the revolution." They were all murdered in less than a week after hastily convened tribunals in which the victims were tried. On January 21, 1793, Louis XVI was tried, sentenced to death and beheaded.

On October 16 of the same year, Marie Antoinette was also

beheaded, without being told of her crime. She bravely faced her executioners. From then on, France ceased to be a monarchy. She was now a Republic and has been so until today. The following were the <u>ten</u> consequences of these events:

1. slavery ended in all of the French colonies
2. price controls for grain and other necessities of life were introduced
3. imprisonment for debts were prohibited
4. the metric system of weights was introduced
5. the law of primogeniture was repealed
6. there were more land reforms
7. there was an attempt to abolish Christianity and to replace it with the worship of reason. This was the direct impact of the Enlightenment. But the attempt failed. By 1794, religion became a private matter. Church and State were separated.
8. a new national calendar was introduced
9. the national army was reorganized
10. Though at war at this time with Britain, Holland, Spain and Austria, France performed well in battle after battle between 1793 and 1796. The French army did well abroad and these victories preserved the homeland from foreign conquest.

In order to ensure these victories, the French leaders "resorted to a bloody authoritarianism … known as the Terror."15 A Committee on Public Safety, charged with the responsibility for wartime emergencies was behind the Terror. This committee had twelve members who were loyal to the Jacobins. The Jacobins claimed to be the disciples of Jean Jacques Rousseau (1712-1778), the famous French philosopher, essayist and novelist.

Rousseau had been famous for his Social Contract theory which advocated that sovereignty be vested in the people. The Jacobins believed that they were the champions of the interests of the common man. There were three notorious members of the Committee on Public Safety: Jean Paul Marat, Georges Jacques Danton and Maximilien Robespierre, with Robespierre being the most famous of the three.

In the last six weeks of Robespierre's influence within the Committee, "no fewer than 1,285 heads rolled from the scaffold in

Paris."16 The Terror lasted from September 1793 to July 1794, just ten months. But, it is estimated that about 20,000 French citizens were murdered in those ten months, an average of 2,000 per month!

Peasants and laborers, rather than the nobles, were by far the main victims of the Terror, including innocent women. Marie Antoinette, their Queen, was one such woman. However, there were <u>three</u> important accomplishments by the Committee on Public Safety, namely:

1. the reversal of the trend toward de-centralization, which had been the nature of the reforms;
2. significant reduction of the pace of industrialization by fostering the interests of the less-privileged, and
3. encouragement of the institution of a class devoted to the ideals of republicanism. France was saved from the coalition of European powers and conquest.

However, the Committee on Public Safety could not save itself. By July 1794, it had virtually lost all friends and support.17 For example, Robespierre and twenty-one of his colleagues were all executed on July 28, 1794. A counter-revolution had begun. In 1795, the National Convention of the Jacobins passed a new Constitution which "granted suffrage to all adult male citizens who could read and write."18

This new Constitution vested executive power into the hands of a board of five men and the board was known as the <u>Directory</u> which ruled France from 1795 to 1799. Also, the new Constitution provided for a Bill of Rights, including a declaration of the duties of the citizen. Unfortunately, the era of the Directory was not very popular since any opposition to it was ruthlessly crushed either by execution or deportation.

In March 1797, the first free elections in France since it became a republic were held. But, in September, the Directory annulled most of the election results of the previous spring season. Hence, in 1799, desperate and facing many uprisings and severe inflation, the Directory asked for assistance from their able and young General, Napoleon Bonaparte (1769-1821), to take charge. This was the beginning of the third stage of the French Revolution.

Actually, the Napoleonic era began in 1804 and would be followed by a series of mini-revolutions of 1830 and 1848, which lie outside the scope of this present study.19 As in Britain in the 1660s, the key issue for the French people was absolutism, which we have already defined.

Napoleon Bonaparte had had a brilliant military career, defeating the British at Toulon in 1793. He was promoted from the rank of a captain to that of Brigadier-General at the age of 24. He had attempted a further victory against the British in Egypt and the Near East.

Also, Bonaparte had remarkable successes in Italy and North Africa. On account of these victories, he became a national hero and was called upon by the Directory to become France's First Consul on November 9, 1799. He held the position, not as king of France, but as a temporary Consul until 1804 when, driven by his ambitions, he crowned himself in the cathedral of Notre Dame, in Paris.

He was now the Emperor Napoleon I, ushering in a new era and dynasty. The leaders of the Revolution must have rolled in their graves as this action signaled the return to the monarchy which had been abolished through much bloodshed. Practically, the French Revolution came to an end with the accession to power of this new but self-confident military autocrat.

Some scholars have included the Napoleonic era (1804-1814) as part of the French Revolution. But in the opinion of this writer, there was really nothing revolutionary about the fifteen years of the Napoleonic regime. Indeed, the era marked the substitution of the monarchy with an autocracy, dictatorship and despotism. Napoleon was no democrat nor libertarian in any serious sense of the meaning of those terms.

Napoleon's era were times of wars, not peace. Fortunately or unfortunately, France lost the island of Haiti, in the Caribbean, under his watch. The Haitians used the logic enunciated under Thomas Paine's "the Rights of Man" to justify their declaration of and war for independence. They succeeded and became the first black nation in the Western Hemisphere.

With Napoleon, there were no great and noble ideals for freedom and human rights. His fame in European history is the creation of European intellectuals, a myth. He ruled France for fifteen years, with the great ambition of being France's self-appointed messiah. Thus, he was a megalomaniac.

At the time, being France's messiah seemed a good idea since the country badly needed a capable leader, one with a sense of confidence, direction, and leadership skills. Later on, this ambition for messiahship became the root cause of Napoleon's downfall. His military setbacks in Canada (1812), in Russia (1812), the one in which France lost 200,000 men, and in Spain (1813), soon eroded his supposed invincibility.

On March 31, 1814, Tsar Alexander I of Russia and King Frederick William III of Prussia successfully invaded Paris. Napoleon knew that he was finished. He was then exiled to the Italian island of Elba. However, to his credit and in less than a year, Napoleon was successfully back to France. But he soon ran out of luck.

On June 18, 1815, he met his next defeat at the battle of Waterloo. Again, he was exiled to the island of St. Helena in the south Atlantic where "he lived out a dreary existence writing self-serving memoirs until his death in 1821."20

It is time to ask ourselves: "What lessons are there for the Africans to learn from the French Revolution?" The author, Jacques Sole, in his book, Questions of the French Revolution: A Historical Overview (1989), attempted to address our question when he contended that "the French Revolution isn't [today] quite what it used to be."21

"For a long time," Sole wrote, "they had an appealing analysis of the great event of 1789 ... The Revolution of 1789 was ... viewed as the victory of the bourgeoisie, backed by the common people, after imprudent provocation by the aristocracy. The resulting new order at first reflected its dual origins, but was soon forced to cope with both the spread of the revolutionary spirit and clashes with the rest of Europe."22

Sole, a graduate from the Sorbonne and a Professor at the University of Social Sciences in Grenoble, as well as the author of several books on European history, raised many questions to help us understand the French Revolution. One such question was about the underlying causes of the Revolution. He argued that such causes were not the triumph of the Enlightenment, but the need to defeat despotism and raise the standard and quality of life of the French citizens.23

Sole noted that "the overall decline in the French standard of living facilitated the outbreak of the Revolution within the context of an economy that was unable to keep pace with a demographic explosion that was throwing society off balance in the cities and the countryside."24

Sole did point out that "eighty percent of all the French at the time of the Revolution were peasants, but they played no role in the events that preceded the fall of the <u>ancien</u> regime."25 The tyranny, oppression and exploitation of these peasants by the Church and State was at the root of the French Revolution.

These factors, as we have seen in all the revolutions considered, will always be resisted no matter how formidable and how long they may exist. Herein lies the lesson for Africans today, who have been terrorized by the State and, who sometimes, have been exploited by the Church. It is even much more painful that the oppressors and exploiters are, by and large, the African leaders themselves who should have learned their lessons from the European colonization of Africa.

As I stated elsewhere, the human heart <u>always craves</u> for decency, the right kind of treatment, human equality and freedom. Africans will need to consider whether we must spill necessary blood in order to obtain and preserve these virtues of equality, justice and freedom. Africans must decide how much blood will have to be shed. Africans will have to learn from Robespierre that "what goes around comes around," as the Americans would say.

In France, absolutism was obliterated as a result of the Revolution. Republicanism emerged. Absolutism must die in Africa. Africans must continue their journey on the road to true democracy by emphasizing their belief that people do have rights and duties of citizenship. The promotion of this ideology will mean the "re-branding" of Africa which can bring the best out of our people.26

The rulers of Africa must learn from both King Charles I of England and King Louis XVI of France that <u>there is always an inherent power of the poor</u> which ought NOT be taken for granted. Gustavo Gutierrez, the South American Professor of Theology and historian John Iliffe of Nigeria had warned us of this.27

Also, African autocrats should be aware of the power of women, who are often the poor ones in the society, and who can turn into revolutionaries when they are aggrieved to a point. The women will not always be silent. They possess tremendous power when well-organized.28

African rulers must not be puerile and foolish, such as the foolishness of marrying so many wives and, in particular, marrying a profligate woman who will arouse the hatred of the citizenry against the leadership. No African leader should marry a woman who despises the people and dares to tell them to "eat cake" when the poverty in the country cries out to the high heavens!

Queen Marie Antoinette of France was Jezebelian in her style and irresponsibility. Public officers who have such wives should get rid of the risk on their hands. The rulers should follow the example of Nelson Mandela whose wife had become too much of a burden for him.

Above all, the enthronement of true national freedoms, human equality, justice and love should be of paramount concern to all of us. The days for royal or monarchical absolutism (super-chiefs) or the so-called divine right of kings must be gone forever in Africa. This is the significance of the French Revolution for Africa and Africans.

THE RUSSIAN REVOLUTION (1917-1953)

Russia, the world's largest country, twice as large as the United States of America or China, lies in the eastern extremity of Europe and Asia. The Russians have always had a history of dictatorships. Their origin goes back to the early Slavs, to the reign of King Vladimir in the tenth century A.D. when Russia was first converted to Christianity.29

Like the English people, the Russians have fought many wars, including the ones against Turkey, Poland, Japan, Germany and France. But like France, they have had a long tradition with monarchical governments going back to A. D. 900. Their rulers were known as the tsars and the last of the tsars was Nicholas II (1894-1917). Revolution followed the last years of this monarchy after many years of the weakening of tsarism.30

The modern state of the Union of the Soviet Socialist Republics (USSR) came into existence in December 1922 and collapsed in 1991. In this discussion, we are concerned with the revolution which occurred during the years of the two Russian rulers, Vladimir Ilich Lenin (1917-1924) and Joseph Stalin (1924-1953).31

Before the emergence of Lenin and Stalin, absolutism characterized Russia's political system, just as it had in England and in France. Tsar Nicholas II was a staunch defender of autocracy. Born on May 6, 1868, he grew up to study under private tutors and was an accomplished linguist. He traveled extensively at home and abroad. In 1890 and 1891, he made a trip around the world.

In military service, he rose to the rank of a colonel. He became emperor on October 20, 1894, upon the death of his father, tsar Alexander III (1881-1894). He continued with the policies of his father. In less than a month after his coronation, he married princess Alix of Hesse-Darmstadt. He was 26 at the time. Historians believe that he was an exemplary husband and a devoted father of five children.

However, Nicholas was a weak ruler who was unconcerned with politics. Herein lay the seeds of his downfall and the eventual end of more than 300 years of Romanov rule in Russia.32 During the second decade of his rule, a mini-revolution occurred in 1905, led by the Reverend Father George Gapon who, with his worker's group of about 200,000, sought relief for their grievances.

On January 22, 1905, a day known as Bloody Sunday," George Gapon's group were fired upon at St. Petersburg and this incident sparked off a revolution. It was an event reminiscent of the French Bastille. It was reported that "merchants closed their stores, factory owners shut down their plants, lawyers refused to plead cases in court, even valets and cooks deserted their wealthy employers."33

On October 30, Tsar Nicholas II realized that the game was up – he had a serious rebellion on his hands. He issued a manifesto that offered guarantees, personal liberties, a promise of moderate, liberal franchise, and affirmed that, in the future, no law would be valid unless it had the approval of the legislature. This was the highpoint of this mini-revolution.

However, between late 1905 and 1907, the tsar issued royal decrees that negated many of the promises which he had made in October 1905. His actions paved the way for further revolutionary action, to be led by Lenin, Stalin, and their Bolshevik colleagues.

In retrospect, the 1905 revolution was not far-reaching for a number of reasons. This is why I called it a mini-revolution. First, the Russian army, which had been fighting against Japan since 1904, remained loyal to its Commander-in-chief, the tsar. It would have been possible, if necessary, for the tsar to have crushed the revolutionaries, had he so desired.

Secondly, there arose a division between the reactionaries and the Octobrists – a group of bourgeosie Russians who believed that the 1905 revolution had gone far enough, especially after the royal promises had been made in October that year. And, thirdly, the workers did not want to continue with the general strike against the government.34

But the 1905 revolution did have some positive gains: Russians became more convinced than ever before that the government was not theirs nor for them. Secondly, the revolution provided the belief that the workers could control the destiny of Russia. Thirdly, more conciliatory reforms were made between 1906 and 1911 in such areas as agriculture, formation of labor unions, land grants, reduced work hours, health and accident insurance.

However, many Russians knew that they were not progressing along the lines of reforms as much as their counterparts in the other European countries and that a new revolution should occur at an opportune time. That time came in February and March 1917, during the third year of World War I. This time, the Russian military had "proved incapable of sustained success in the [battle] field."35

Vladimir Ilich Lenin was the key leader of the 1917 revolution.36 Born on April 22, 1870, at Simbirsk, Russia, his father Ilya Nikolaevich Ulyano was a successful official in public education and worked for a progressive democracy and a free universal education. Thus, he was a nobleman, not a peasant. Lenin's mother, Maria Alexandrovna Ulyanova, was a housewife.

Scholars now believe that Lenin came from a mixed ethnic background that included Jews, Germans and Swedes. In 1886, when Lenin was 16, his father died of cerebral hemorrhage. The next year, his eldest brother, Alexander Ulyanov, was executed for being involved in a terrorist bomb plot to kill Tsar Alexander III, the father of Nicholas II. As he grew up, Lenin attended Karzan University to study law.

Lenin was a bright student and was greatly influenced by the German philosopher Goethe whose works he read, but it was Karl Marx who touched his heart most deeply. Due to his student activism and political ideas, he was expelled from the university on December 4, 1887. He studied on his own while, at the same time, he read many more books by Marx, including Das Kapital. In 1891, he was admitted to the Bar, after passing his law examinations.

Also, Lenin knew Latin, Greek, German and English. He had graduated first in his law class and practiced in St. Petersburg. Soon, he was more and more involved in underground Marxist activities. He married Nadezhda Krupskaya, a Socialist activist, at the age of 28. On December 7, 1895, Lenin was arrested for his activism and imprisoned for 15 months. He was exiled to Siberia at this time.

A hard-working man, Lenin wrote and published his book, The Development of Capitalism in Russia in April 1899. He was 29. His exile came to an end in 1900, the following year, and he then traveled throughout Russia and western Europe. At one time, he lived in Zurich and Geneva (where he studied and lectured at the city's State University).

Lenin also visited Munich, Prague, Vienna, Manchester, and London. He co-founded a newspaper in Switzerland called Iskra, or "The Spark," with Julius Martov and wrote many articles and books related to revolutionary causes. Through those writings, Lenin rose to a position of influence and power among his fellow Social Democrats.

He was very engaged in the Russian Social Democratic Labor Party (RSDLP) and by 1903, was the leader of the Bolshevik faction of the Party. Three years later, he was elected to the Presidium of the RSDLP but, due to his political activities, he self-exiled himself to Europe to avoid another arrest. He was in Europe until the early days of the 1917 Revolution.

Lenin's years in Europe began in 1907. Hence, for ten years, he read and studied revolutionary ideas. He settled first in Finland for security reasons. In 1909, he published another book, Materialism and Empirio-Criticism. This book became fundamental in understanding the Marxist-Leninist philosophy. In 1912, he attended the Prague Party Conference.

When World War I began in 1914, Lenin opposed it as an "imperialist war" and split with the Second International (1889-1916), which he had been a member since 1905. The Second International was an organization of socialist and labor parties formed in Paris on July 14, 1889. It was responsible for the declaration of May I as International Workers' Day and March 8 as International Women's Day. One of its achievements was the 8-hour working day throughout the world.

Lenin was briefly detained by the Austrian authorities but he returned to Berne and Zurich on September 5, 1914. He attended the Zimmerwald anti-war Conference of 1915. In 1916, he published yet another book which he titled, Imperialism: The Highest Stage of Capitalism, in which he argued that western imperialism promoted profit maximization on a global scale.

Lenin seemed to have been surprised when the 1917 Revolution began. He decided and determined to return to Russia as quickly as possible. He did so on April 16, 1917 and settled first in the city of Petrograd. The revolution began when the steel workers of St. Petersburg went on strike in March and thousands of people poured out into the streets. The power of the tsar collapsed and the legislature (the <u>Duma</u>), then led by Alexander F. Kerensky, took over power.37

Lenin clearly saw his role in this Revolution. Through many of his publications, which came to be known as the "April Theses," he called for an uncompromising opposition to the Kerensky Provisional government. On the other hand, the Kerensky government accused him and his colleagues of being German paid agents. The accusation did not stick.

In July, the Bolsheviks failed in a coup attempt, thereby forcing Lenin to flee again into Finland. There, he released a new book, <u>State and Revolution</u> (1917), in which he called for a new form of government based upon the Council of workers. Successfully, he returned to Petrograd to inspire the October Revolution. He was 47, about the age of President Barack Obama.

In two days, November 6 and 8, 1917, Lenin directed the overthrow of the Kerensky government. By November 8, the Bolsheviks and Lenin were completely in control and power. He was elected Head of State in Russia. Thus, **by the use of the power of the pen and of the intellect, coupled with careful strategic planning, Lenin acquired great political power**.38 This ought to be a lesson for any young person in search of political power.

However, Lenin did not single-handedly bring about the 1917 October Revolution. His "ablest and most prominent lieutenant was Leon Trotsky (1879-1940)."39 Born in the Ukraine of middle-class Jewish parents, Trotsky had been exiled to Siberia for his role in the 1905 Revolution. He escaped but, later, had his political dreams sabotaged by Joseph Stalin after Lenin's death on January 21, 1924.

A "fiery commander of the Red Army,"40 who believed like Lenin in world revolution against capitalism, Trotsky was unable to convince his countrymen and women with his message of the overthrow of global capitalism. Instead, Stalin's campaign of a nationalist policy of building up socialism at home prevailed over Trotsky's.

Stalin had Trotsky and his supporters disgraced publicly. In 1927, Trotsky was expelled from the Communist Party. In 1929, he was again expelled from Russia. In 1940, Trotsky was murdered in Mexico by Stalin's henchmen.41 All this makes one to wonder if Stalin had become Lenin's counter-revolutionary. With Trotsky eliminated, Stalin consolidated his political base and ruled Russia dictatorially until 1953.

Stalin was born on December 18, 1878. He was "the son of a peasant shoemaker in the province of Georgia."42 He began his education at a theological seminary. In 1895, at the age of 17, he was expelled for lack of a religious vocation. He then turned his attention to revolutionary activities.43

He worked hard to rise to the enviable position of the General and First Secretary of the Central Committee of the Communist Party of the Soviet Union from April 3, 1922 to March 5, 1953. By March 6, 1941, he was already the Chairman of the Council of the People's Commissars, virtually the Head of State.

We can now ask the questions that are uppermost on our minds, namely, "What was the Lenin-Stalin Revolution all about? Was it necessary and what did it achieve? What made it revolutionary and, much more importantly, should Africans emulate that Revolution or not?" Luckily for us, the historian John M. Thompson, in his book, Revolutionary Russia 1917, published in 1981, has some answers for us.

Thompson contended that the February 1917 Revolution signaled the "collapse of the Old Order,"44 the end of absolutism and monarchical government in Russia. When more than 200,000 workers poured out into the streets of Russia on March 8-10, 1917, Nicholas II unwisely sent out his soldiers to quell the strike.

"Police and troops opened fire on demonstrators ... killing more than one hundred "45 people. Nicholas's Prime Minister tried to dissolve the Duma but that effort was strongly resisted by the president of the Duma. And, Nicholas II paid no serious attention to those developments, as Commander-in-chief.

On the evening of March 12, "it was all over" as "the tsarist ministers were soon arrested by a revolutionary committee, and the central authority of the old government simply disappeared almost without a trace. It was a complete and cherished victory for the people"46 of Russia. The casualties in Petrograd numbered just about 1,400.

Thompson wrote that the "February Revolution was neither unexpected nor inevitable; but it was indeed sudden and elemental."47

Also, he maintained that four factors brought about the revolution, namely, Russia's disastrous involvement in World War I, the disorientation of its society, the people's sense of injustice, and the collapse of the economy.48 Tsar Nicholas II, a well-traveled ruler, did not learn any lessons from the French, English or the American revolutions.

We may now state that what Lenin and his Bolshevik colleagues achieved in March 1917 was the complete destruction of the monarchy in Russia. But, in October, they turned their attention to the Kerensky Provisional regime , the remaining remnant of the old Order.

According to Thompson, the Kerensky administration had become "a necessary evil, tolerated by many but not enthusiastically supported in any quarter."49 Many Russians tolerated the government because their country was still at war. But the government was vulnerable to an overthrow. "The October Revolution was not inevitable ... the demise of the Kerensky regime some time in the near future would have been hard to avert."50

Lenin and his Bolshevik colleagues took advantage of the weaknesses within the Kerensky central government and plotted a coup for their selfish interests. "By November 8 the Bolsheviks had overthrown the central government in Petrograd and controlled the capital."51 The rest of Russia soon fell into their hands.

Thompson added: "The unlikely revolution had been made and won." But, although Lenin, Trotsky, Stalin and their colleagues had won, a terrible Civil War "broke out in the middle of 1918," a few months after the cessation of hostilities between Russia and Germany.53 Therefore, many Russians believed that their revolution (particularly the February Revolution), had been hijacked and betrayed.

According to another historian Sheila Fitzpatrick, the Russian Civil War was between "Bolshevik 'Reds' against anti-Bolshevik 'Whites'."54 Thus, the Civil War became Lenin's preoccupation for more than nearly three years. He had become the new autocrat, to whom all Russians obeyed or perished.

A new secret Police Force was introduced to protect the Lenin-despotic government. Censorship was quickly imposed upon Russians. Lenin himself faced many assassination attempts. Two of these happened on January 14 and on August 30, 1918. In reaction to these attempts upon his personal life, Lenin ordered the murder of 200,000 people, same number that began the revolution.

These killings came to be known as "The Red Terror"55 of 1918-1921. More killings followed during the rule of Joseph Stalin who had suggested the idea to Lenin in the first place. On the positive side, the Bolsheviks provided a program of agricultural collectivism. Also, there was a five-year industrialization plan for which, under Stalin, an estimated 20 million Russians paid with their own dear lives.56

Moreover, the Russian government played a decisive role in the defeat of Adolf Hitler of Germany in 1945. Consequently, Russia emerged as a superpower. In about six pages of his book, Thompson provided what he called "the significance of the Russian Revolution."57

First, according to Thompson, Lenin emphasized socialism and his government introduced "state capitalism" or an "inverted socialism"58 imposed from the top down. Lenin also completed what was lacking in socialism because of his implicit faith in the idea.

Secondly, Lenin offered the idea of a democratic socialist revolution which purported to advance the interests of the toiling masses and workers. But, in actuality, his idea frustrated the personal hopes and dreams of the people. Thirdly, Thompson observed that the Russian Revolution offered a modernizing pattern (never mind the purges!) for other countries like China, Turkey, Cuba, Bolivia, and Ethiopia. But we should always ask, "at what human cost?"

Thompson concluded that "... in many ways the promotion of the Russian Revolution remains unfulfilled."59 Yes, unfulfilled and I ask, "did the Russian Revolution end tyranny, absolutism, inequality, and economic exploitations? Did it provide for social justice, freedom and human rights, a decent livelihood for all, and a life with human dignity?"

Truly, the revolution DID NOT work out as was expected. One must remember Stalin's 20 million people who perished at his hands. One must also remember the 200,000 who perished under Lenin. **The Russian Revolution cost more than 20 million lives! Was it worth it?** Is Russia today a paradise, an El Dorado?

Professor Fitzpatrick, already cited, stated that "the legacy of the Russian Revolution"60 pointed to the establishment of the Communist Party, the collective farms, the five-year and seven-year plans, and the division of the world into two camps: socialistic and capitalistic.

Fitzpatrick also added: "This was the great revolution of the twentieth century, the symbol of socialism, anti-imperialism, and rejection of the old order in Europe."61 I am very astonished that it was seen as a "great revolution" of the 20th century. What a misconception! Change by a very bloody process.

Fitzpatrick believes that the Russian Revolution offered a hope of freedom from oppression to some people and a definition of socialism to others – a socialism that hinged on the seizure of state power and its use as an instrument of economic and social transformation.

Other historians believe that the results of the Russian Revolution "were profound" and that "no other regime in the history of western Europe had ever attempted to reorder completely the politics, economy, and society of a vast nation as the Russians had in the short space of twenty years."62

By 1932, 70% of Russia had been industrialized. But, I insist that we must NEVER forget the high price for that industrialization: state-sponsored terrorism, murder of millions of innocent fellow citizens, slave-labor camps, unrelenting indoctrination and brain-washing, persecution of innocent people, trampling upon human and civil rights, atheism as a state religion, and an unquestioning loyalty to the state.

It seems to me that the soul of Russia was lost in its mad pursuit of modernization. Education became a tool of the Revolution. So were intimidation, violence and mind-control of the population. Stalinism institutionalized tyranny as much as the tsars before it had done.

It is, therefore, not surprising that Nicolas Berdyaev, in his book, The Origin of Russian Communism (1999), observed that:

> Lenin was an imperialist and not an anarchist; his whole thought was imperialist, despotic... He read a great deal and studied much, but he had no breadth of knowledge or great intellectual culture. He acquired knowledge for a definite purpose, for conflict and action.63

Berdyaev pointed out that Russian messianism was like Jewish messianism.

This analysis of the Russian Revolution under Lenin and Stalin has great lessons for Africans. First, the analysis shows us how not to do the revolutionary thing. Every human culture has a history of anti-oppression and a hunger to be truly free from the menace of absolutism.

Therefore, if the Africans must have a revolution, and they will, the true African revolutionaries must be vigilant over the possibility of betrayal and the hijacking of their cause. Africans DO NOT need the Lenins and Stalins of Europe who would not care to butcher millions of our dear people for personal power and aggrandizement. We have already witnessed what the Nguemas, Mengistus and the Mobutus may do to their own people.

As I have stated in the previous chapters of this book, Africans must constantly ask themselves: how many million lives would they be willing to sacrifice so that true freedom and equality may reign? Is it possible for the Africans to sustain their freedom after the revolution and for how long?

Also, would the Africans be willing to play the game of placing political ideology over some fundamental issues of life? And, whose ideology will guide the revolution: Lenin's, Stalin's or Jeffersonian? Is there a home-grown African ideology that may be used to guide the revolution?

Africans must also seriously consider the cult of personality worship which often arises during any revolution. This issue borders around the quality of the character of the African revolutionary leaders. Who will be such leaders and from what schools of thought will they emerge? These are important questions for the coming African revolution.

In the words of the historian Orlando Figes, Africans must yearn for "a glorious February ... expressed in the national uprising that overthrew the old regime," and "expressed in the universal effort to establish freedom and to defend it against both internal and external foes ... Such high expectations"64 must never be allowed to be dashed by selfish reactionaries and megalomaniacs.

THE CHINESE REVOLUTION (1927-1950).

On July 26, 2007, The Washington Times declared on its front-page headline: "China Becomes the Growth Engine: U. S. Dislodged As World's Pace-setter."65 This report went on to say that China, for the first time in 2007, had dislodged the United States from its long reign as the main engine of global economic growth, with its more than 11 percent growth eclipsing the sputtering U. S. growth of about 2 percent.

This Chinese economic miracle did not come overnight and its political transformation did not also happen overnight. China, the world's most populous country, with an estimated 1.3 billion people in 2006, is the principal nation in Asia, next to India. They are both nuclear weapons-owning countries. Like the ancient Egyptians, China had a dynastic history which lasted back to 1600 B.C.

According to the author Bamber Gascoigne, there had been eight major dynasties in China which went through many revolutions.66 These revolutions included the Xinhai or Republican Revolution (1911-1912); the Second Revolution (1913); the Constitutional or Third Revolution (1917-1922); the National or Northern Expedition Revolution (1926-1928); the Communist or Civil War Revolution (1927-1950); and the Cultural Revolution (1966-1976).

Academic scholars on China are unsure whether the Tiananmen Square protests of 1989 constituted a revolution. But what is clear to us is that modern China began around 1912 when the Republic of China was proclaimed. That revolution brought to an end the Manchu Dynasty which had ruled China for many centuries.67 In this discussion, we are concerned primarily with the revolution which was ushered in by the emergence of Chairman Mao Tse-tung (1893-1976).68

When one examines the nature of political developments in China, it is safe to say that China had <u>never</u> had a history of democracy and freedom. China's monarchical past was based upon autocracy and dictatorial regimes similar to the absolutisms in Europe which we have examined already.69 So, in order to understand modern China, one must understand Chairman Mao and the revolution which he led.

There are many good biographies about Mao but we will draw largely from the book, <u>Mao: The Unknown Story</u> (2006), written by Jung Chang and Jon Halliday.70 According to these two authors, Mao was born on December 26, 1893, in the city of Shaoshan, in the province of Hunan. His father was Yi-Chang who was born in 1870.

In order to pay off family debts, Yi-Chang became a soldier. But Mao did not love his father because Yi-Chang was a strict disciplinarian who often struck his young son. Yi-Chang could not stand his son's idleness. In 1968, Mao suggested that he would not have cared if his own father was among those tortured to death.

However, Mao dearly loved his mother because she spoiled him. She was from the Wen clan of Shaoshan and did not receive a personal name because of the custom of those days. She married Mao's father when she was only 18 and Yi-Change was 15. She was a devoted Budhist and gave her husband three children, two of which died in their infancy. It is no wonder that his mother indulged Mao as the sole survivor of her three children.

The family gave Mao the name "Tse-tung." "Tse" means "to shine on." "Tung" means "the East." Thus, Mao's full name meant "to shine on the East," and it expressed the hope that the family placed upon him.71 Mao grew up a troubled child who, in his mid-teens, gave up Budhism which he had accepted because of his love for his own mother.

Mao was raised in the Confucian school of classics up to the age of 18. He had private tutors and seemed to have done well in Chinese language and history. He had a passion for reading. But even at ten, he had become rebellious toward his tutors and was expelled three times from school. He did not do well in mathematics. He was "hopeless at economics."72 In 1907, he was expelled by his fourth teacher.

At 14, Mao got married to a bride who was four years older than him. Her family name was Luo. She died in 1910 just three years after they had wed. This brief experience turned Mao into an antagonist of pre-arranged juvenile marriages. He seemed to have had the same kind of marital experience which Mahatma Gandhi had. Mao later referred to these kinds of marriages as "indirect rape." At the age of 16, he wanted to leave home to attend another school twenty-five kilometers away.

At the new school, science, world history, geography and foreign languages were taught. It was a modern school and was located in the city of Changsha, the capital town of Hunan province. It was there that Mao learned about America and Japan which had defeated Russia in 1905. He did not like the peasant life of his village. Therefore, at 17, he bid goodbye forever to his village and left for Changsha, a cosmopolitan city.

Mao arrived at Changsha just about the time when the Republican Revolution of 1911-1912, which ended the imperial rule in China, was in the making. Soon, he took sides with the revolutionaries for the overthrow of the Manchus. The Manchu Dynasty was regarded as representing "foreign" domination because they were not Han Chinese who were the majority of the population.

Somewhere between 1911 and 1920, Mao became a confirmed communist.73 He wrote his first essay on the topic and pasted it up on a wall of his school. This action was in line with the custom at the time. The Republican Revolution began around October 1911 and a new Republic of China was proclaimed on January 1, 1912. The new military leader was Yuan Shih-kai. He became president but died four years later in 1916.

A civil war erupted after the death of Yuan Shih-kai and Mao enlisted into the army. However, he quit after a while and returned to school for further study. He quit school again after only six months and tried to self-study at the local provincial library. He read many western authors and all kinds of new books. Reading helped free his mind of the constraints of tradition and custom.

Quite likely, Mao was rebellious because of his unhappy upbringing and his early marriage experience. Because his father, at this time, had threatened to cut him off from any kind of support, he returned to school. He registered at a local Teacher's Training College in the Spring of 1913, at the age of 19. There, "the students were exposed to all sorts of new ideas and were encouraged to think freely and organize study groups."74

Here, Mao intensified his interest in socialism and communism. The Teacher's college was located near the Xiang River, Hunan's largest river. Mao was free to develop his own ideas and thoughts which became the core of his life's philosophy.

From his earliest expressions and writings, one finds that Mao believed in the burning of <u>all</u> past literature which related to the Tang and Sung dynasties. One scholar refers to the Tang dynasty as representing the "Golden Age" of Chinese civilization.75 Yet, Mao did not find anything good with that dynasty. He believed in "the destruction of Chinese culture."76 This kind of mindset signaled what he would do were he to become prominent in China.

In 1917, at the age of 24, much of Mao's ideas and thoughts had been formed and his mind was made up. For example, he wrote as follows:

> I do not agree with the view that to be moral , the motive of one's action has to be benefitting others. Morality does not have to be

defined in relation to others… People like me want to … satisfy our hearts to the full, and in doing so we automatically have the most valuable moral codes. Of course there are people and objects in the world, but they are all there only for me.77

Mao's ethical perspective and morality stated above come close to hedonism and egoism. But furthermore, Mao also wrote as follows:

People like me only have a duty to ourselves; we have no duty to other people. I am responsible only for the reality that I know and absolutely not responsible for anything else. I don't know about the past. I don't know about the future. They have nothing to do with the reality of my own self. Some say one has a responsibility for history. I don't believe it. I am only concerned about developing myself… I have my desire and act on it. I am responsible to no one.78

As we can see, Mao did not seem to believe in anything unless he could personally benefit from it. He may have been a victim of his early childhood poverty and life of hardship. He wrote that "absolutely selfishness and irresponsibility"79 lay at the root of his outlook on life. In this he was honest, at least, to himself. He enjoyed violence and destruction when he expressed the following view:

Giant wars will last as long as heaven and earth and will never become extinct…The ideal of a world of Great Equality and Harmony … is mistaken. … Long-lasting peace is unendurable to human beings.80

From the above citation, it is obvious that Mao did not regard war as a cause for human misery and pain. Under his rule, millions of the Chinese people starved to death, but it did not concern him since he bore no responsibility for his actions. His revolutionary ideology was summed up in two words: violence and destruction.

In order to bring about fundamental change, Mao expressed the next view as follows:

The country must be… destroyed and then reformed. … This applies to the country, to the nation, and to mankind. … The destruction of the universe is the same… People like me long for its destruction, because when the old universe is destroyed, a new universe will be formed . Isn't that better?81

Here, evidently, Mao was playing God and he was speaking as if he was the creator of the universe. There is a string of messianism in his voice just as we saw in the Russian messianism under Lenin. This worldview of Mao stayed with him for the remainder of his 60 years of life. Recent studies on leadership would agree that Mao was not a true leader but a megalomaniac personified! Ironically, this was the man who led China at the time.

In June 1918, Mao graduated from the Teacher's Training College unto unemployment. He was 25 at the time. His friends tried to travel abroad, but Mao could not travel to France because he could neither speak French nor Russian. Therefore, he decided to travel to Peking where he lodged with seven other friends in three tiny rooms. There, he found work as a junior librarian. This assignment did not last for long.

Some scholars believe that we can best understand Mao in terms of the process by which China came to be a key player in world politics. These scholars believe that there were four stages of the Chinese Revolution, namely:82

1. Yuan Shih-kai, from 1912-1916
2. the era of the warlords, from 1916-1928
3. the national era, from 1923-1948
4. the Communist era, from 1949-1976.

Antecedent to the emergence of the Communists was a man known as Dr. Sun Yat-sen (1866-1925) who was regarded as the Father of the Chinese Revolution through his ideas and many writings. In 1912, he had been involved in the overthrow of the monarchy. His political party was known as the Guomindang.

Dr. Yat-sen had a great influence upon Mao. Betrayed in 1913, Yat-sen fled to Japan. But upon his return to China, he traveled to Peking at the invitation of one of the warlords in 1924. He, however, died of liver cancer the following year.

Another influence upon the life of Mao was Chiang Kai-shek (1887-1975), a young General of the Guomindang. A leader among the Nationalists, Chiang Kai-shek was passionately anti-communist and determined to wipe them out completely.83

The Guomindang influence lasted for only 20 years. The "Soviet-

Guomindang alliance ended in 1927."84 And, following the termination of the alliance, the communists began to wax their political and military muscles in China.

These communists had been driven underground but soon began to build up their influence owing to the personal abilities of Mao. In 1921, he had been one of the twelve men who founded the Chinese Communist Party (CCP). Two years later, he rose to be the leader of the radical wing of the Guomindang. He was its Deputy member in the Central Executive Committee, who was entrusted with the task of peasant organization.

Thus, Mao was close to the people but he earnestly believed that "whoever won the peasants would win China."85 It was no surprise that he would become the man that led China from 1949 to 1976. Mao's concept of a revolution was expressed in the following words:

> A revolution is not the same as inviting people to dinner. A rural revolution is a revolution by which the peasantry overthrows the feudal landlord class... Several hundred million peasants will rise like a tornado or tempest, a force so extraordinarily swift and violent that no power, however great, will be able to suppress it.86

Chinese communism differed from Russian communism. The Chinese communists formed village cooperative associations to aid the poor; destroyed temples and burned the wooden idols for fuel; and intimidated and assaulted the "bad gentry."87 When the forces of Chiang Kai-shek nearly wiped out the communists, Mao and his colleagues were forced into the infamous "Long March" of 1934-1935, in which 71,000 of them died.

The long trek was "a mass migration across 6,000 miles of difficult terrain."88 Mao emerged from these circumstances as the head of the CCP, destined to rule China. Like the English Fabians, Mao believed in the tactic of "retreat in order to advance."89 In 1937, the small number of 9,000 communists of 1935 had risen to over 40,000.

The key programs of Mao, which appealed to the peasants and his party, were:

1. rent reductions
2. establishment of land banks and cooperatives

3. building of irrigation works
4. education of peasants in better ways of cultivation
5. crop control
6. a call for national resistance against Japanese aggression
7. equitable tax structures
8. anti-corruption measures
9. political indoctrination
10. guerilla warfare against the Nationalists and the Japanese invaders.90

The main weaknesses of the Chiang Kai-shek government aided Mao's cause and the communists won in three areas:

1. the confidence of the civilian population
2. relief for the common people
3. posing as saviors of the revolution.

In the civil war that ensued, the communists won and forced the Nationalists to flee into Taiwan in 1949. On October 1, 1949, Mao had publicly declared the founding of the People's Republic of China before a crowd of 300,000 people at the Tiananmen Square in Peking. Mao was now fully in charge. "By 1950, the jurisdiction of President Chiang's government was confined to the island of Taiwan."91

A 30-year struggle for the economic transformation of China began. The Communist Revolution had come to stay. What did they achieve? They brought about some sweeping and far-reaching economic, social, political and cultural changes which have ushered in the China that we know of today. In 27 (1949-1976) years, Mao and his government introduced:

1. heavy industries
2. savings extracted from the peasants
3. capital investments
4. agricultural developments which doubled in output between 1949 and 1969
5. reforestation
6. building of dams and reservoirs

7. mineral productivity in such areas as oil produce, coal, gas, manganese, tungsten, antimony, tin, copper, and aluminum.
8. fertilizers, steel and electricity
9. railroads, the first of which had come to China in 1875
10. automobiles and jet planes, including electronic, surgical, and scientific instruments.

The "Democratic Dictatorship"92 of Mao Tse-tung had brought some fundamental changes but it was all materialistic, without soul or spirit. The rapid modernization of China followed. "At ten minutes past midnight on the morning of 9 September 1976, Mao Tse-tung died."93 And, now, we may ask: "At what human cost did China achieve its present greatness and power?"

First, a land reform which dispossessed many of the landlords claimed the lives of about one million Chinese people. These landlords were often shot when they appeared accused before a People's Court. The authors Chang and Halliday wrote that Mao was "responsible for well over 70 million deaths in peacetime."94

I had earlier cited Dr. D. James Kennedy who, in 1994, stated that Mao killed "about 72 million human beings from 1948 to 1976."95 How do we feel reading that? [Even Idi Amin of Uganda never killed that many people and western propaganda made much noise about him!] A poem composed in 1964 in honor of Mao expressed the messianism in the Chinese Communist Revolution, and read as follows:

> China has produced a Mao Tse-tung He seeks happiness for the people. He is the people's great savior.96

As far as Africa is concerned, we ought to ask some important questions regarding Mao's Revolution, such as: "What are the lessons we can learn from this analysis? Should African communist rulers blindly lead us along the same alley?"

First, if they want a revolution (and they will surely have one), Africans must understand that the antidote to an evil, tyrannical, totalitarian government is GOOD GOVERNANCE. There is no other substitute. Mao and his colleagues inherited centuries of monarchical, brutal regimes that did not care for their people. When the communists arrived, they were hailed as the best of many evils. After all, they gave to the people the much needed bread and butter.

Second, the qualities or characteristics of an emerging charismatic leader can be discernible if the citizens would pay close attention to the belief system of the emerging leader. People heard and read the views of Mao when he was a nobody but they paid little attention. But Mao was quite clear about his views.

He had said that he cared for no one and that he was not responsible to anyone. He could therefore murder 72 million of his own people and the world went on as if nothing had happened to human rights. Contrariwise, no African ruler has ever killed that many people. One wonders what Mao would have done to his foreign enemies whom he may have despised. Did Hitler kill that many Germans in addition to six million Jews?

Thirdly, emerging African revolutionaries must be vigilant and decide whether 72 million human lives or more would be necessary to be eliminated in order to have a truly revolutionary change. How precious are the African lives and whose life would be sacrificed?

These are not easy questions to answer. We can learn and answer our questions from this study of world history. Or, do we want to repeat the mistakes of history? This book has been written to avert such a colossal and horrifying mistake.

CHAPTER EIGHT
Decolonization –
Africa's First Modern Revolution

For more than 500 (1415-1915) years, the enemies of African freedom had supposed that they had a divine right to invade, conquer, rule and dominate the lives of African people. Also, they believed that it was their God-given right to exploit and expropriate the continent. They dared to call their mission to Africa "the white man's burden."1

The Europeans, who had made their entry into Africa, did so first as "explorers," then traders, missionaries, and colonialists. They imposed their political rule, worldviews, and religion upon the Africans through military conquest. Thus, the tiny islanders who call themselves British, for example, came to believe that the sun never sets upon English soil.

While attending High School from 1962-1966, we used to sing, ignorantly though, that "Britania shall never be a slave." That was one of the songs of colonialism in Nigeria. In 1945, some of the Europeans did not think that the Africans would ever regain their lands, minerals, independence, and sovereignty.

Many Europeans held the belief that Africa was their "New World." So, they renamed some African cities and territories, such as Rhodesia, Pretoria and Lagos. Even Nigeria was a name provided by a foreign British woman. When independence came in 1960, "Senegal had a European population of over 30,000, the Ivory Coast about 20,000, and Madagascar 40,000."2

Kenya, Rhodesia (now Zambia), and South Africa (which ought to be called Azania) had their "permanent" white settlers who never thought that they ought to go home, back to Europe. South Africa had more than a settler population. European Dutch immigrants who had arrived there in the 1650s, contrived an evil, oppressive, political system of government called apartheid which was used against the Africans.3

From 1415, when the city of Ceuta in Morocco was invaded and captured by the Europeans, to 1885, when the Berlin Conference for the "scramble" for Africa ended, Europeans took time to collect intelligence reports about Africa, as they developed their own military hardware, technologies, and prowess.

When they had convinced themselves that they could vanquish the Africans, the Europeans then embarked upon unholy wars to conquer and colonize Africa. There was nothing peaceful nor civil about the enterprise. Africans were <u>militarily</u> subdued and subjugated. The white conception that Africans were docile and ready for conquest remains only a myth of the white mind.

Meanwhile, Africans were used as objects for trade for profit, in what came to be known as chattel slavery. The slave "trade" was primarily for the enrichment of Europe and the economic development of the so-called "New World" territories. There was nothing Christian nor philanthropic about it. It is idiotic for anyone today to think that white people were doing Africans a favor by enslaving them!

Beginning from 1619 to 1865, a period lasting for nearly 250 years, the transported Africans to the Americas worked from sunup to sundown as beasts of burden, hewers of wood and drawers of water, without pay or salaries, but subjected to the most barbaric and cruelest inhuman treatments. Common sense should have dictated that the slaves be treated better for working for the slave-masters free-of-charge. But it was not so.

The Africans on the continent constantly were harassed, kidnapped, and "sold" for profit for the Europeans until 1830 when good sense and reason returned to the Europeans. Really, it was the advent of the European Industrial and Scientific Revolutions which actually made white slavery untenable. But, slavery and colonialism dealt terrible blows to the economic, political, social, religious, and intellectual advancement of Africa.

Anyone who believes otherwise is either demented or downright dishonest. Because of this long period of time, 545 years of European domination over Africa, it is not surprising that some professional white scholars like Peter Duignan, L. H. Gann, and David K. Fieldhouse reached the erroneous conclusion that colonialism was beneficial to the Africans.4 I wish to God that their descendants would someday become the colonized!

The Europeans did not reckon with some socio-political forces, like the First and Second World Wars, which brought their empires to an end and impelled the Africans to engage in the process of decolonization. In this chapter, I intend to try to define the term, decolonization, and I shall contend that, properly understood, decolonization was Africa's first modern revolution. After 75 years, it is time to have another continental revolution.

There are many definitions of, as well as works on, decolonization. The world-renowned Nigerian economist, Dr. Adebayo Adedeji, wrote that: "We define 'decolonization' as the dismantling of colonial institutions and the minimization of foreign control and power." He added: "Decolonization is not a gift from the imperial powers; it needs the initiative of the oppressed."5

The historian James D. Le Sueur, who was an Assistant Professor at the University of Nebraska-Lincoln, defined decolonization as follows:

> As a matter of definition, … I take decolonization to mean (almost without exception) a process during which hard-won battles were waged between nationalists and metropolitan colonial powers.6

The above definition supports Adedeji's contention that decolonization was not a gift; it was not a favor which the European colonialists did for the Africans. Dare anyone say that Nelson Mandela spent more than 27 years in jail for the gift of independence and freedom for black South Africans!

Another school of thought says that decolonization is "a process where a colonized people, by developing a consciousness based on the remnants of the traditional culture, redefine themselves as peoples and reassert the distinct qualities that historically guided their existence."7

Professor Prasenjit Duara, in his book, <u>Decolonization: Perspectives From Now and Then</u>, (2003) sees decolonization as the political struggle for legal sovereignty as well as social movement for moral justice and political solidarity against imperialism, both formal and informal, and external and internal.8 However, in 1970, Crawford Young, in an essay he titled, "Decolonization in Africa," offered no definition of the term.9

Thus, in general, the accepted definition for decolonization is the action of changing from colonial to an independence status. It is a process to liberate, set free, or grant independence to a former colony. <u>The American Heritage Dictionary</u>, published in 2000, and updated in 2003, states that decolonization is to free a colony from its dependence status.

In his book, <u>The Wretched of the Earth</u>, which had been cited earlier on, Fanon discussed the various forms of decolonization. He contended that decolonization reflected a violent phenomenon ... adding that "the naked truth of decolonization evokes for us the searing bullets and bloodstained knives which emanate from it." Fanon was writing from the context of the Algerian War of independence.

Reacting against Fanon, a South African journalist Mandisi Majavu argued that Fanon was wrong by implying that every time there was a "political violence," then decolonization was taking place. In an angry tone, Majavu stated that Fanon was "talking nonsense," since decolonization did not, and indeed, does not have to be violent.

Majavu contended that violence is not necessary nor is it sufficient on its own to bring about decolonization. He believed that the goal of decolonization was independence from colonial rule. Furthermore, he argued that to have the Congolese people believe that the enthronement of Mobutu's regime upon them represented decolonization would be a false conceptualization of the term.

Majavu noted that Fanon said nothing about **transformation**, the vital ingredient needed in the decolonization process. According to Majavu, decolonization includes "a change in the system – meaning, a replacement of oppressive and dehumanizing institutions by liberatory ones."10

Majavu insisted that decolonization was "actually a transformation of the system," which may include peaceful means and negotiation; but which does not necessarily include violence. My question is: "what do you do if the colonizer would not peacefully negotiate? What, if there was no hope, as in apartheid South Africa, that the regime there would ever transfer power to the colonized? Does one remain in servitude ad infinitum?"

To be sure, there were several methods by which decolonization was effected. These methods included African resistance to military occupation, nationalism, Pan-Africanism, social mobilization and political organization, which led to civil disobedience, like what Gandhi did in South Africa and in India. Sometimes, there were boycotts, labor strikes, riots, and unfortunately, wars for freedom or independence.

A combination of methods were used in the cause of decolonization. Hence, author Jeremi Suri, in his book, Power and Protest (2003), contends that the actions against colonialism were a kind of protest which brought about the rise of détente. The actions were also some sort of a global revolution against imperialism.11

Many scholars have gone on to examine and analyze those methods that led to decolonization.12 But it must be stated that decolonization derived its impetus from the experiences of the Africans who had served in the colonial military abroad in the two World Wars and had changed their sense of white invincibility. They had seen many whites die on the battlefields, like the Africans. The aftermath of the wars dealt a great blow to the previous and strange perception of white people.

Moreover, those Africans who had studied abroad were determined to change things when they got home to Africa. One such student was Dr. Nnamdi Azikiwe (popularly referred to as Zik of Africa), who returned to Nigeria and eventually, in 1960, became its ceremonial Head of State.13 Similarly, Kwame Nkrumah returned from the United States to become Ghana's first Prime Minister when the country became independent in 1957.

Theo Ayoola was a Nigerian recruit in the British colonial army stationed in India in 1945. In a letter which he wrote to Herbert Macaulay, who, at the time was considered the father of Nigerian nationalism, Ayoola said: "We have been told what we fought for, ... That is freedom. We want freedom, nothing but freedom."14

Another source of inspiration which aided decolonization was the U. S. President Woodrow Wilson's notion of the Fourteen Points which expressed the idea of self-determination for colonized peoples everywhere. And, President Franklin D. Roosevelt's idea of the Four

Freedoms, namely, freedom of Speech and expression, freedom of religion, freedom from want, and freedom from fear, inspired the African nationalists.15

Between 1945 and 1960, the revolution of decolonization fully engaged the attention of the world community and practically brought the European empires to an end. We should not forget the Civil Rights Movement led by Martin Luther King, Jr., which began about the same time. That movement did give hope and inspiration to African freedom fighters.

Personally, I agree in part with Mandisi Majavu when he said that the most significant aspect of decolonization ought to have been the **transformation** (if any) which decolonization should have brought to the Africans. For in hindsight, Africans seem <u>not</u> to have been humanly transformed at the beginning of the post-colonial era.

In part, I do not agree with Majavu when he suggests that armed resistance was not necessary in the decolonization struggle. Africans had no choice but to fight the European intruders anyhow. Just as colonialism had a great negative impact upon the Africans,16 it is incumbent upon us to reflect upon and understand how decolonization transformed the lives of Africans for the better.

In the light of what has happened in Africa since 1960, and is happening to many Africans in this post-colonial era, especially in the area of national politics and human rights, I wonder if we can talk of any human transformation unless we consider the matter of the quality of African life. Is kleptocracy in Africa helping us to be better off or not?; that is the question.

Having said this, however, I believe that we ought to be asking many questions regarding the transforming role of decolonization upon Africans. One reason is that, in some quarters, **some Africans do believe that the colonialists were far better than our fellow African bureaucrats!**

For example, I lived through the days when the Nigerian postal system was superb. Ask any Nigerian today how great is our Nitel and Nipost. We need a national survey that tells us about the national mood regarding our African governments. These governments would be shocked to discover that the average African has no faith nor trust in his or her government. So, where are the dividends of decolonization?

For me, the answers to these kinds of questions are what matter the most in our discourse. With regard to human freedom and true liberty, we should be asking how free are the Africans since the coming of decolonization. We ought to examine the qualitative and quantitative benefits of decolonization since 1960. Some experts have already pronounced the verdict: Africa has fallen far worse today than during the dying years of colonialism. But, why?

I believe that one of our probing questions ought to be: "Have we Africans fared better or worse since our black brothers and sisters took over the reign of power and governance? In Nigeria, I have personally overheard people complain and wish that the British were back to govern them. Is this not an indictment on us?

If a scientific poll on this issue were conducted by an internationally independent organization, many African governments would score an "F" grade. This would be an interesting revelation. But, I also believe that such a discovery would help us move better in the right direction. Perhaps, our nationalists had labored and died in vain.

I would like to believe and hope that African independence from European colonial rule had some benefits and hereunder are some of my reasons for hope:

1. The opening of the doors to racial pride and self-esteem
2. Advancement in the social, political, economic, and intellectual capital of the Africans.17
3. The emergence and growth of a nationalist culture.18
4. The opportunity and right of Africans to govern themselves, to make their own mistakes, correct such mistakes, and to learn from such mistakes. The tragedy is that so far, our rulers tend to play God; they refuse to learn from their mistakes and from history. They are very proud, arrogant, incorrigible and adamant.
5. The emergence and growth of many African national and international institutions such as the African Union (AU), the African Parliament, the Economic Community of West African States (ECOWAS), the African Development Bank (ADB), and several other similar institutions. It should not be forgotten that prior to independence, there were no such institutions, talk less of African owned airlines and shipping companies.

6. Hope in the increasing economic wellbeing of the African individuals.
7. Spiritual elevation of the Africans, particularly in terms of contextualization and exegesis
8. Ability to challenge the assumed "universal" norms and worldview from the West and to elevate the African worldview.

Since decolonization, many African leaders have emerged, leaders who could not have emerged under colonial rule, leaders who someday could be internationally renown, leaders like Nelson Mandela and Kofi Annan, the former Secretary-General of the United Nations Organization (UNO).

The significance of decolonization is that it gave room or birth to a New Africa, an Africa of revolutionary character. No longer would the African be seen as inferior to the white man or woman, subservient or a person in perpetual servitude to the white world.

Decolonization reversed this world order and brought a new sense of human equality and dignity. This was the beginning of the rising of the sun for the people of the African world, a sun which will never set until Africans, worldwide, are fully emancipated. Decolonization was a real revolutionary change after more than 500 years of the Western domination of the Africans. It was the beginning of the opening of the doors to racial self-esteem.

Now, the African has the opportunity and right to rule himself and his people. Independence meant an end to taking orders and instructions from London, Paris, Berlin and Belgium. At the least, in theory, this was supposed to be the case. Africans were to develop their own national budgets, see to the economic, political and social advancement of their own continent, and contribute to the civilization of mankind.

One other thing that is not often stated is this. Decolonization placed an awesome responsibility on African leaders to lead in humility and righteousness and service. It was probably a divine act which brought us all out from the house of slavery. But today's African leaders have almost totally forgotten the Grace of God that brought them through. What do we expect next but nemesis and retributive justice!

More than 50 years after independence, some of us Africans really wonder what Africans have contributed to world civilization except in becoming the world's gigantic consumers of products from elsewhere and accumulators of external debts. I wonder whether our so-called leaders have lived up to the responsibilities of true leadership. Many of our leaders are very much tied to the apron strings of the ex-colonialists and jump whenever they sneeze.

Another benefit of decolonization has been the ability of many African intellectuals to challenge those assumed Western worldviews which the West regarded as universal but which, really, were not so and were inimical to the improvement of the intellectual and social capital of the Africans. In this post-decolonization era, few Westerners would freely denigrate the African and get away with it without counting the cost of their actions. The days of the Tarzan syndrome are nearly gone.

In point of fact, open acts of racism in the United States are on the retreat. Racial segregation, prejudices, lynching, and homophobia are no longer publicly applauded. There are, though, pockets of anti-blackness. But, by and large, those who still engage in derogatory practices against the African should be aware of the costs for their actions. The days of public lynching of a black person because he is black are over.

Although the Africans have embraced the two foreign religions – Christianity from the West and Islam from the East – they do not remain as observers but as actors in these religions. In fact, Africans have successfully indigenized and Africanized the two religions. Some of the largest congregations of either Christianity or Islam are headed by Africans. This is a far cry from the days when such heads or leaders were always white and foreign.

It is my earnest hope that the day will soon come when an African will sit as head of the papacy in Rome or in the futuristic St. Paul's Catholic Cathedral in Abidjan's Ivory Coast, in West Africa. One may think that this will be impossible. But world events have their ways with revolutionary changes.

A hundred years ago, who ever thought that African women would be serving as ambassadors in Washington, D.C. where African slaves were paraded for sale? Who ever thought that a black man would become a U. S. President only 143 years after the Civil War? Who ever thought that black men and women in America would ever be on a mission to the moon?

Apart from the changes which decolonization has brought, Africans ought to be eternally grateful to the men and women who fought so that better days would be here again for the African. In this respect, we are deeply grateful to author Raph Uwechue who, in his trilogy, <u>Makers of Modern Africa: Profiles in History</u> (1991), documented "some 680 life histories of eminent Africans … who in their various ways,"19 contributed to the decolonization exercise.

In particular, we mention people like Julius Nyerere of Tanzania, Jomo Kenyatta of Kenya, Obafemi Awolowo of Nigeria, Leopold Senghor of Senegal, and Kenneth Kaunda of Zambia. The late Oliver Tambo of South Africa also deserves a special mention for his struggles against apartheid. Because of these heroic men and women, decolonization was accomplished.

As far as I am concerned, decolonization was Africa's first modern revolutionary achievement. We Africans ought to celebrate it with pride. For, without it, many of us would have continued in colonialism up until today. We owe our nationalists a great debt of gratitude. We ought to eternally remember them just as the Jews remember Moses. We ought to study their roles and lives in the course of the history of our fatherland.

CHAPTER NINE

*Preparing Ourselves For The
Coming African Revolution*

Now that we have come close to the conclusion of this book, let me share with you some concrete things which I believe we should be doing in preparation for the coming African revolution. In motivational speaking circles, we say that success is 99% preparation.

GET READY.

First, we must get ready for the coming revolution. The Jewish Rabbi, Jesus Christ, taught about the importance of counting the cost in readiness for a major action. He told two stories and illustrations to make His point. The first story was about a builder who, if he is sensible, must first ask himself how much a proposed real estate project would cost before starting to build.

Such a builder would be mocked if, for some reasons of lack of sufficient funds, he is unable to complete the project. The wise builder must first conduct his feasibility and viability research before starting to build. In His second story, Jesus spoke of the readiness of a king who wants to go to war.

No king, Jesus said, would go to war without first considering the military might of his opponent's army. Otherwise the opponent could humiliate such a king by a victory that was not anticipated (Luke 14: 28-32). Preparation and readiness involve thorough research

, assessments, feasibility, and planning our course of action. Always, we must remember the words of Mao, "A revolution is not a dinner party."

Another aspect of preparation is the avoidance of unnecessary blunders and mistakes. Careful preparation will reduce the incidence of such mistakes. They say that practice makes perfect. Have you ever seen any serious athlete who refuses to practice become a champion? Preparation minimizes the fear of failure and of anxiety. Africans who want fundamental changes must get ready and be prepared.

Preparation also means doing the right or good thing. A student who does not prepare for an examination is likely to fail the test. Preparation is imperative. Just building the team necessary for a great project or cause of action is a very important part of the preparation process. It is during preparation that one may build the needed team necessary for a revolution. It is at this point that one may discover who are the persons of the same mind for action.

In practical terms, the African people who are preparing for the coming revolution must <u>read</u> all they can about revolutionary movements, including this book. **No modern revolutionary action can be successful out of gross ignorance!** A prospective revolutionary must read everything about what it takes to effect a socio-political change and volunteer as an intern in such programs which would enable him or her to lead.

Take for example Dr. Martin Luther King, Jr. (1929-1968), at the age of 30, traveled all the way to India to get a firsthand knowledge of <u>Satyagraha</u>, Gandhi's philosophy of nonviolence. He went there in 1959 because he wanted to prepare himself for the Civil Rights Movement which opened the doors for his leadership.

In West Africa, Nnamdi Azikiwe and Kwame Nkrumah traveled abroad to study hard so that they would eventually return to lead their people toward independence from colonial rule. In the Bible, Joshua was an apprentice to Moses, and Elisha was the protégé for Elijah. No one should ever want to be a leader without first being a servant of the people. Today's Africans must educate themselves in the arts and sciences of revolution.

HAVE CONVICTION.

A revolution is never made out of fickle-hearted men and women. A revolution requires men and women of convictions. The people of the African Revolution must be people who are convinced that their cause is just and redemptive. They must whole-heartedly believe in the revolution. In fact, they must be willing to die for the revolution.

Wishy-washy kind of people or those with no backbone are no good for a revolution. "A rolling stone gathers no moss," people say. The world of revolutionary leadership should not include people without convictions. Think of Margaret Thatcher of Britain. She was not popularly called the "Iron Lady" for nothing. She was full of passion for her ideas.

Indira Gandhi of India and Golda Meier of Israel were not spineless leaders, either. When Mahatma Gandhi returned from England after his law studies, he wanted to practice law in South Africa. But, he was soon convinced that social engagement, not law, was to be the more important call in his life. When the immortal John Brown took up guns against American slavery, he was convinced of the justness of his cause and actions.

When William Lloyd Garrison formed the American Anti-slavery Society in 1833, he eloquently declared war on slavery. He was persuaded and convinced that he needed to fight this cause with everything in him. There would be no retreat from his cause. He received numerous death-threats, insults, humiliations, and persecutions from pro-slavery white enthusiasts. But his mind was made up because he had conviction.

Revolutions are not made out of jokesters! The reason why modern-day revolutionary attempts are not successful in Africa is primarily because most of the people have no real convictions. There is a terrible climate of apathy throughout the land. There are few (if any) people who are tenacious enough to take a stand on anything. There are not enough Steve Bikos and Nelson Mandelas.

BE COMMITTED.

Next to conviction is the issue of commitment. But, what does commitment mean? The dictionary uses several words to define the meanings of the terms commit and commitment. These include trust, taking charge, to carry into an action deliberately, perpetrate, obligate, pledge, relegate, confide, consign, and an agreement. Commitment is an obligation to be responsible and never to waver. I repeat, it is the precursor to ACTION, a stage.

Study the lives of all great men and women like Gandhi, Moses, Jesus, Mandela, Marx, Madam Currie, and Shakespeare. Study the lives of Martin Luther King, Jr., and the German reformer, Martin Luther. The quality of commitment is prevalent in their lives. They are the kinds of people who start something and finish it.

In a previous book on the indispensable qualities of visionary leaders, I discussed this matter of commitment.1 But, here, let me just summarize it for you. Commitment means to stand tall and steadfast in the face of adversity, even if no one else walks the walk with you. It demands focus and the absence of distractions. There is no quitting from the cause. Quitters never win and winners never quit.

Commitment is a pledge to perform, follow through, and complete a task. Commitment is like leading your soldiers across a bridge into battle, burning up all your bridges behind you, and resolving to conquer or to be conquered. Commitment involves a determination which never wavers. In the Bible, Esther was a woman of conviction and commitment.

When faced with a situation that involved the lives of her dear people the Jews, Esther decided to break a royal norm or tradition and went into action. Her last words before seeking the king's favor were: "IF I PERISH, I PERISH." (4: 16).

Edison tried to invent the electric light bulb. He experimented for 9,999 times. Even his wife tried to persuade him to give up! But, on the 10,000ᵗʰ time, Edison succeeded with his scientific revolution. But for Edison, There would be no electricity. Patience, conviction and commitment brought the revolutionary change.

It is conviction which produces commitment. Committed people are often stubborn or resolute people. When the early disciples saw that their master Jesus had actually risen from the dead, they went out committed to global evangelism to turn the world the right-side up. They were ready to give up their very lives and counted their lives as nothing. Such are the kinds of people needed for the African revolution. Such people cannot be bought nor bribed to abandon a cause.

TAKE ACTION.

You must execute the revolution, that is, you have to take action. Talk is cheap. But, actions make the difference. You have to give wings to your convictions and fly, that is, implement your project – even the revolution. All ideas, concepts, and notions about any kind of revolution will do us no good until there is ACTION or performance. Action is the visible evidence or expression of your convictions and commitment. A familiar advertisement in the U. S. says: "JUST DO IT."2

Author William Feather has been quoted as saying that "an idea isn't worth much until a man is found who has the energy and ability to make it work."3 Actions speak louder than words. If you want to see changes in your country and continent, you must not wait for some angels to descend from heaven to cause the change to happen.

You must be the angel for revolutionary change. This was precisely what King David did for Israel. He killed Goliath and brought change to his country. And, that is what Africa badly needs today – men and women of action.

EVALUATE AS YOU PROCEED

Azikiwe, the first president of the Federal Republic of Nigeria, once said that no condition is permanent. He was stating the obvious. As you take action for a revolutionary cause, you must also be ready and willing to evaluate or review the processes and changes that have occurred.

There is no guarantee that one method used in a revolution will be the most perfect all the time. Therefore, you must constantly review and revise your plans. Listen Africans: if you do not have the room for evaluations and reviews (they call these in business quality assurance) your actions may soon become obsolete or static. Life demands changes and you will soon be willing to accommodate change and make some necessary adjustments.

Why do so many African leaders stay put in office until they are booted out in a violent coup-de-tat? I believe one reason is because they are often resistant to change. Knowing that they had failed their people miserably, or thought they had a divine right to stay on, they refuse to go. They often presume that they know it all and are indispensable. This is sheer arrogance and stupidity.

Just as you and I want change, so will others want changes to our revolutionary actions. If we pretend that there is no one else better than us, then we are self-deceived, idiotic, and our day of calamity will be just around the corner. This is the hard truth which most African rulers do not want to hear. Their sycophants have done a good one on them.

In 2007, Frederick Chiluba, the former Zambian president, was found guilty of stealing $46 million by judge Peter Smith of a London High Court. Chiluba appealed. But on August 17, 2009, the Associated Press reported that he was acquitted of corruption charges in Zambia after six years of trial. His wife, Regina, had been sentenced in March for three and half years, with hard labor; but she also appealed.

Chiluba once was reputed to have been a born-again Christian but would to God that he had wise counselors who would have reminded him that the day of shame was around the corner. He had replaced Kenneth Kaunda but did not seem to be ready for change. Chiluba had ruled Zambia for ten years.

PRAY FOR THE REVOLUTION

Perhaps, you are surprised that I have included prayer as an important element in the process of effecting an African Revolution. Don't be surprised. It has been said that more great things are achieved in this world through prayers than we are willing to acknowledge.4 If not so, then why do we often pray, even instinctively?

Let me assure you that we are more than material objects. We are made up of body, soul and spirit. Our souls and spirits are the areas of our being that respond to the supernatural realm, in spite of our daring attempts to suppress our spiritual experiences. You have to admit that there are some things that human reason alone cannot decipher.

Few people have ever seen an angel; but does that mean that they do not exist? How did we even come to invent such a word like angel? Spiritual things are not against logic; they are beyond logic. The things that belong to the supernatural world have to be supernaturally discerned. The Bible says so and I agree.

In our efforts to effect a revolution, we must ardently pray for its success as we work towards it. More than anything else that we have to do, we must pray for divine guidance and wisdom. We must seek divine guidance as Gideon did in the ancient land of Israel. I believe that there are already many Gideons all over Africa. But they must persist and persevere to have a heart and burden like Gideon did.

In the history of Israel, we learn that there was once a man called Gideon (Judges 6-8) who lived when times were hard and precarious. Some scholars have dated the period as between 1491 B.C. and 1095 B. C. This was between the death of Joshua and the ministry of prophet Samuel.5 For seven years (6: 1), an enemy country called Midia ravaged the emergent nation of Israel and rendered life hopeless for many of the Jewish people.6

The important thing to remember here is that the Israelites sought divine help. They prayed for a revolution (6: 7) and God answered them through an angelic appearance to one of them called Gideon. At the time, Gideon was busy on his farm (6: 8-23). Gideon was instructed to attack his enemies with only 300 soldiers! The miracle was the defeat of the Midianites with this small number of 300 men.

We should note that before the battle, Gideon had complained that Israel felt forsaken by their God. They forgot that they had sinned terribly against their God. Similarly, many Africans, including those in the diaspora, feel that God has certainly abandoned us. He has left us into the hands of both domestic and foreign oppressors and exploiters. Hence, we desperately need a revolution.

But, in truth, God loves us, too. We need to consider the help which comes from the Creator of the whole universe. Since, for about half a century, our efforts to govern ourselves properly have failed woefully, and Africa is now in a deplorable condition, we ought to pray earnestly for divine help and work diligently toward a revolution. When our God responds and we act, as Gideon did, Africa will be free and blessed, indeed.

CHAPTER TEN
Conclusion

Those who make peaceful revolution impossible will make violent revolution inevitable.

— U. S. President John F. Kennedy, 1962

In this very important and powerful book, I have sought to define the term revolution, with the hope that the ordinary man or woman would understand it and so cease to be frightened by it. Also, hopefully, by gaining an understanding of what a revolution is and the benefits that can be derived from a wisely planned and executed one, leaders and non-leaders alike will not feel threatened by those who advocate revolutionary changes.

As we have seen, part of the meaning of the word revolution involves fundamental changes in the society. Since life involves growth and change, we should not be afraid of change and growth. We have dared to state that major changes began in the celestial realm. The Christian Bible claims that, at the beginning of history, there was war in heaven. The origin of revolutions began in that celestial realm before they were transferred down here on earth.

Over the years and centuries of recorded history, there have been many revolutions and, I am sure, there will be many more and more revolutions even when man ceases to exist. Therefore, the African should embrace the idea of revolution. The only thing to fear is what sort of revolution we will embrace. Hence, in Chapter Five, I have examined and analyzed five different kinds of revolutions. We must reflect on them carefully.

The necessity for an African Revolution has been examined in Chapter Three. Given our current levels of corruption and political incompetence, which have led to dissatisfaction among the ordinary Africans, our leaders ought NOT be surprised that our continent is ripe for revolution. Indeed, we are over-ripe for the inevitable coming revolution.

Here, my aim is to make available the different choices and routes frequently traveled, routes we can take with dire consequences. We can no longer fain to be ignorant. I have not endorsed any option or route. That decision will have to be made by the Africans themselves, But I pray that they make the right choice and decision.

Also, in the light of African religious leanings, I have included a chapter which I call, "Theological Basis for African Revolution," keeping in mind that we ought to be, in the words of Dr. Vernon C. Grounds, "insurrectionists" for God. We should remember that God may not pour down fire and brimstone upon us in order to awaken us to recoil from our unrighteousness.

But, God does have some remnants of humanity whom He can use to stop us from committing suicide as a result of our terrible evil ways and actions. The forces of Nyerere once had to stop Mobutu from committing more barbarism. Therefore, we must be willing to learn from history's six major revolutions. The wise heed a warning while the foolish often walk right into a pit with their eyes wide open.

I have argued that decolonization was Africa's first modern revolution — a process by which our nationalists overthrew and destroyed the twin evils of slavery and colonialism. This is my interesting original thought and contribution to the discourse on decolonization. It is a useful model for all who are dissatisfied with the current state of affairs in Africa. If it was good to overthrow white evil against us, it is much more excellent to demolish black-on-black evil.

Above all else, the ordinary people of Africa must prepare themselves for the coming revolution and not be overtaken unawares. The stubborn fact is that either we wisely engage ourselves in needed reforms or forces outside the continent will bring the revolution to us by way of a re-colonization of Africa. That will be another kind of revolution in the historical epoch of Africa. The enemies of Africa are watching us.

I end this book with the solemn words credited to the former U. S. President, John F. Kennedy when, on March 12, 1962, he warned the visiting Latin American diplomats gathered at the White House that "those who make peaceful revolution impossible will make violent revolution inevitable."1 Earnestly, I pray that Africans will heed his warning.

Notes

Introduction

1. See Musikilu Mojeed, "Achebe Calls for Revolution in Nigeria," 234Next.com (June 9, 2010).
2. See Ikenna Anokute's writing in SSalvucci@Mathematica.mpr.com and in the New York naijawriters of 2009.
3. See Sulaimon Olanrewaju, "Conditions for a Revolution in Nigeria," Nigerian Tribune (April 4, 2008).
4. Ibid.

Chapter One: A Definition for Revolution

1. Mao cited in Rana Mitter, A Bitter Revolution: China's Struggle With the Modern World (Oxford: Oxford University Press, 2005), 242 and also, Selected Works of Mao Tse-tung, vol. 1 (Beijing: n.p., 1975), 28. For other works on Mao and his revolution, see Jung Chang and Jon Halliday, Mao: The Unknown Story (New York: Anchor Books, 2006), 15; John King Fairbank, The Great Chinese Revolution 1800-1985 (New York: Harper and Row, 1987), 41-42; and Roderick Macfarquhar and Michael Schoenhals, Mao's Last Revolution (Cambridge, MA: The Belknap Press, 2006), 290-291.
2. Mao cited in John Bartlett, Familiar Quotations (Boston, MA: Little, Brown and Co., 1980), 826.
3. Crane Brinton, The Anatomy of Revolution (New York: Random House, 1965), 3.
4. Ibid., 25.

5. Hannah Arendt, <u>On Revolution</u> (New York: Penguin Books, 1965), 21. See also her other impressive book, <u>The Origins of Totalitarianism</u> (New York: Schoken Books, 1976). It was first published in 1948.

6. Arendt, <u>On Revolution</u>, 23.

7. Ibid., 25.

8. Ibid.

9. Ibid., 28.

10. Ibid., 29.

11. Ibid.

12. Ibid., 21-58.

13. Arendt cited in Vernon C. Grounds, <u>Revolution and the Christian Faith</u> (Philadelphia, PA: J. B. Lippincott Co., 1971), 19.

14. Karl Marx cited in Michael Lowy, <u>The Theory of Revolution in the Young Marx</u> (Chicago, IL: Haymarket Books, 2005), 93-94. For other works on Marx, see Neil J. Smelser, ed., <u>Karl Marx on Society and Social Change With Selections by Friedrich Engels</u> (Chicago, IL: The University of Chicago Press, 1973), Saul K Padover, <u>Karl Marx: An Intimate Biography</u> (New York: New American Library, 1980), David McLellan, <u>Karl Marx: Selected Writings</u>, ed., (Oxford: Oxford University Press, 1977), and Francis Wheen, <u>Karl Marx: A Life</u> (New York: W. W. Norton and Co., 2000). See also Harold J. Laski, <u>The Communist Manifesto</u> (New York: New American Library, 1967).

15. Grounds, <u>Revolution</u>, 19.

16. Ibid.

17. Ibid., 17.

18. Ibid., 18.

19. Ibid.

20. Ibid.

21. Ibid.

22. Ibid., 19.

23. Ibid., 20.

24. See Bernard Bailyn, <u>The Ideological Origins of the American Revolution</u> (Cambridge, MA: Harvard University Press, 1977), Forrest McDonald, <u>Novus Ordo Seclorum: The Intellectual Origins of the Constitution</u> (Lawrence: University

Press of Kansas, 1985), and Charles A. Beard, <u>An Economic Interpretation of the Constitution of the United States</u> (New York: The Free Press, 1941, 1913).

25. Grounds, <u>Revolution</u>, 20.

26. Ibid., 21-22.

27. Ibid., 17.

28. Ibid., 21.

29. Ibid., 23.

30. Emma S. Etuk, <u>NEVER AGAIN: Africa's Last Chance</u> (Bloomington, IN: iuniverse, Inc., 2008), 246-247.

31. Marx cited in Grounds, <u>Revolution</u>, 18.

32. Thomas Kanza, <u>Africa Must Change: An African Manifesto</u> (Cambridge, MA: Schenkman Publishing Co., 1978).

33. John Henrik Clarke, <u>Who Betrayed the African World Revolution? And Other Speeches</u> (Chicago, IL: Third World Press, 1994). See also his other book, <u>My Life in Search of Africa</u> (Chicago, IL: Third World Press, 1999).

34. Emma S. Etuk, <u>Destiny is Not A Matter of Chance: Essays in Reflection and Contemplation on the Destiny of Blacks</u> (New York: Peter Lang, 1989), 17-28.

35. Neither Eric Hobsbawn nor Will and Ariel Durant, in their books, have any helpful definitions of the term revolution, in spite of their marvelous contributions on the subject. See Eric Hobsbawn, <u>The Age of Revolution 1789-1848</u> (New York: Random House, 1996) and Will Durant, <u>Rousseau and Revolution, vol. 10</u> (New York: Simon and Schuster, 1967).

CHAPTER TWO: ORIGIN OF REVOLUTION

1. Vernon C. Grounds, <u>Revolution and the Christian Faith</u>, 71-104 and 107-122. See also Billy Graham, <u>The Jesus Generation</u> (Grand Rapids, MI: Zondervan Publishing House, 1971), 13-22 and 109-118.

2. Mitter, <u>A Bitter Revolution</u>, 242.

3. See Tom Skinner, <u>Words of Revolution: A Call to Involvement in the Real Revolution</u> (Grand Rapids, MI: Zondervan Publishing House, 1970).

4. Edmund Burke cited in John Bartlett, <u>Familiar Quotations</u>, 374.

CHAPTER THREE: THE NECESSITY FOR AN AFRICAN REVOLUTION

1. Vernon C. Grounds, <u>Revolution and the Christian Faith</u>, 31-32.
2. Emma S. Etuk, <u>LISTEN AFRICANS: Freedom is Under Fire</u> (Washington, D.C: Emida International Publishers, 2002), 86.
3. See Franz Fanon, <u>The Wretched of the Earth</u>, trans. Constance Farrington (New York: Grove Press, 1963).
4. Fanon cited in Grounds, <u>Revolution</u>, 39.
5. Fanon, <u>The Wretched of the Earth,</u> 1963 ed., back-cover.
6. Fanon, <u>Toward the African Revolution: Political Essays</u>, trans. Haakon Chevalier, (New York: Grove Press, 1964), 101.
7. Ibid., 102.
8. Ibid., <u>The Wretched of the Earth</u>, 316.
9. Barry Rubin, <u>Modern Dictators: Third World Coup Makers, Strongmen, and Populist Tyrants</u> (New York: New American Library, 1987), 182.
10. Clarke, <u>Who Betrayed the African World Revolution,?</u>
11. Ibid., 14-15.
12. Ibid., 15.
13. Ibid., 12.
14. Ibid., 12-13.
15. Ibid., 13 and 19-57.
16. See Wilson Jeremiah Moses, <u>The Golden Age of Black Nationalism 1850-1925</u> (New York: Oxford University Press, 1978).
17. See the slave narratives by Francis Bok, <u>Escape From Slavery: The True Story of My Ten Years in Captivity – and My Journey to Freedom in America</u> (New York: St. Martin's Press, 2003) and Mende Nazer, <u>Slave: My True Story</u> (New York: Public Affairs, 2003).
18. Graham, <u>The Jesus Generation</u>, 110-111.
19. Etuk, "Hollow Promises of 'Never Again,': The Genocides of Rwanda and Darfur in a Disengaged and Callous World," An Unpublished Research Paper Presented at Howard University,

Washington, D.C., dated April 4-7, 2007, pp. 4-5. See also Etuk, <u>Listen Africans</u>, 28-33.

20. Elton Trueblood, <u>Declaration of Freedom</u> (New York: Harper and Brothers, 1955), 53-70.

21. Begin cited in Etuk, <u>Listen Africans</u>, 53-54.

22. This story was provided by the Nigerian <u>Daily Sun</u> newspaper dated March 28, 2007. See also Ardo Hazzad, "Nigeria: Muslim Pupils Kill Teacher over Koran," <u>Naijanet.com News Headline</u>, March 21, 2007, and Kola Oyelere et al,, "Bloody Day in Kano," The <u>Nigerian Tribune</u> dated April 18, 2007.

23. Thomas Paine cited in Etuk, <u>Listen Africans</u>, 221.

24. See Efraim Karsh, <u>Islamic Imperialism: A History</u> (New Haven, CT: Yale University Press, 2006), John Esposito, <u>The Islamic Threat: Myth or Reality?</u> (New York: Oxford University Press, 1992), and Robert Spencer, ed., <u>The Myth of Islamic Tolerance: How Islamic Law Treats Non-Muslims</u> (Amherst, NY: Prometheus Books, 2005).

25. Barrington Moore, Jr., <u>Reflections on the Causes of Human Misery and Upon Certain Proposals to Eliminate Them</u> (Boston, MA: Beacon Press, 1969) and Robert H. Hartman, ed., <u>Poverty and Economic Justice: A Philosophical Approach</u> (New York: Paulist Press, 1984).

26. See James H. Cone, <u>God of the Oppressed</u> (Minneapolis, MN: The Seabury Press, 1975) and John Iliffe, <u>The African Poor: A History</u> (New York: Cambridge University Press, 1987). See also Gustavo Gutierrez, <u>The Power of the Poor in History</u> (Maryknoll, NY: Orbis Books, 1984).

27. Thomas Paine cited in Etuk, <u>Listen Africans</u>, 201.

28. Ibid.

29. Ibid., 201-202.

30. See Webster's Seventh <u>New Collegiate Dictionary</u>, 1971 ed., 369.

31. Ibid., 512.

32. This story was reported by Albert Akpor in the Nigerian <u>Vanguard</u> newspaper dated March 30, 2007.

33. This story was reported by Anayo Okoli in the Nigerian <u>Vanguard</u> newspaper dated March 30, 2007.

34. This story was published by Christopher Isiguzo in the Nigerian This Day newspaper dated March 30, 2007.
35. This story is derived from www.allAfrica.com internet source dated March 30, 2007.
36. Ibid.
37. See Desmond Tutu, No Future Without Forgiveness (New York: Doubleday, 1999), 255-282.
38. Cited in George B. N. Ayittey, Indigenous African Institutions (Ardsley-on-Hudson, NY: Transnational Publishers, 19991), 124. See also Simon Kolawole, "Mr. President, Nigeria is Going Down," This Day (July 18, 2009) and Temple Chima Ubochi, "Nigeria is Burning With Wars on All Fronts, Nigeriaworld. com (August 15, 2009).

CHAPTER FOUR: THEOLOGICAL BASIS FOR AFRICAN REVOLUTION

1. W. T. Purkiser, Richard S. Taylor and Willard H. Taylor, God, Man. & Salvation: A Biblical Theology (Kansas City, MO: Beacon Hill Press of Kansas City, 1977), 14.
2. Ibid.
3. Ibid., 16.
4. Ibid.
5. Grounds, Revolution, 71-104.
6. Ibid., 107-122.
7. Ibid., 187-230.
8. See the bibliography in Vernon C. Grounds's book cited above.
9. Galbraith cited in Etuk, What's So Good About Christianity? Five Amazing Ways the Gospel Has Influenced and Blessed Our Lives (Washington, D.C: Emida International Publishers, 2000), 113.
10. Pericles cited in Etuk, What's So Good About Christianity?, 82.
11. Skinner, Words of Revolution, 11.
12. David L. Clough and Brian Stiltner, Faith and Force: A Christian Debate About War (Washington, D.C: Georgetown University Press, 2007).
13. See David Kinsella and Craig L. Carr, ed., The Morality of War: A Reader (Boulder, CO: Lynne Rienner Publishers, 2007).

See also Priye Sunday Torulagha, "A Study of Moral Norms Concerning War in Pre-colonial Traditional Nigerian Societies," Ph.D. diss.,The University of Oklahoma, Norman, Oklahoma, 1990 and Okon Effiong Attah, "The Role of African Soldiers in Politics: New Directions in Comparing Civilian and Military Regimes," Ph.D. diss., Washington University, St. Louis, Missouri, 1989.

14. See Kai Nielson, Ethics Without God (Amherst, NY: Prometheus Books, 1990).

15. Gustavo Gutierrez, The Power of the Poor in History, 117-122.

16. L. E. Toombs, "Ideas of War," in George Arthur Buttrick, ed., The Interpreter's Dictionary of the Bible, vol. 4 (Nashville, TN: Abingdon Press, 2000), 796-797.

17. J. W. Wevers, "Methods of War," in Buttrick, The Interpreter's Dictionary, 803.

18. Chaim Herzog and Mordecai Gichon, Battles of the Bible: A Military History of Ancient Israel (New York: Barnes and Noble, 2006).

19. See Joshua chapter Six.

20. L. E. Toombs, "Ideas of War," The Interpreter's Dictionary, 800.

21. Grounds, Revolution, 83.

22. Ibid.

CHAPTER FIVE: FIVE KINDS OF REVOLUTIONS

1. D. James Kennedy and Jerry Newcombe, What if Jesus Had Never Been Born? The Positive Impact of Christianity in History (Nashville, TN: Thomas Nelson Publishers, 1994), 233.

2. Ibid., 234.

3. Ibid., 235.

4. Ibid.

5. See Chang and Halliday, Mao: The Unknown Story, 15, Maurice Meisner, Mao Zedong: A Political and Intellectual Portrait (Malden, MA: Polity Press, 2007), 5-16 and Mitter, A Bitter Revolution, 110-117.

6. Kennedy, What if Jesus, 235.

7. Ibid.

8. Betty Schechter, The Peaceable Revolution: The Story of

Nonviolent Resistance (Boston, MA: Houghton Mifflin Co., 1963).

9. Ibid., 226-245.

10. Ibid., 226.

11. Louis Fischer, Gandhi: His Life and Message for the World (New York: New American Library, 1982), 9 and Emma S. Etuk, The Indispensable Visionary: Turning Your Dreams into Realities (Washington, D.C: Emida International Publishers, 2006), 55-60.

12. Schechter, The Peaceable Revolution, 24.

13. Etuk, The Indispensable Visionary, 58.

14. Ibid., 64.

15. Schechter, 145.

16. Ibid., 149.

17. Etuk, The Indispensable Visionary, 75-76.

18. David J. Garrow, Bearing the Cross: Martin Luther King, Jr., and the Southern Christian Leadership Conference (New York: Random House, 1988), 108-112. See also Martin Luther King, Jr., Why We Can't Wait (New York: The New American Library, 1963), 15-26.

19. Fantu Cheru, The Silent Revolution in Africa: Debt, Development and Democracy (London: Zed Books Ltd., 1993) and John Perkins, A Quiet Revolution: The Christian Response to Human Need… A Strategy for Today (Waco, TX: Word Books, 1976).

20. Perkins, A Quiet Revolution, back-cover.

21. Ibid., 215.

22. Ibid.

23. Ibid.

24. Ibid., 217-224.

25. Ibid., 219.

26. Perkins, A Quiet Revolution, back-cover.

27. Dr. Chris Ngige, the former governor of Anambra State of Nigeria, is quoted as saying: "We must go into a quiet revolution and that revolution has to be for a good leadership." See Habib Aruna, "I'll Return to Power With Popular Mandate," Daily Independent (Online edition) dated April 9, 2007.

28. Harold H. Titus, Marilyn S. Smith, and Richard T. Nolan, <u>Living Issues in Philosophy</u> (New York: D. Van Nostrand Co., 1979), 430 and 433.

29. See John S. Mbiti, <u>African Religions and Philosophy</u> (Garden City, NY: Doubleday and Co., 1970), 38. See also Eric O. Ayisi, <u>An Introduction to the Study of African Culture</u> (London: Heinemann, 1972) and Paul Thomas Welty, eds., <u>African Cultures</u> (Philadelphia, PA: J. B. Lippincott Co., 1974).

30. See Raziel Abelson, "History of Ethics," in Paul Edwards, ed., <u>The Encyclopedia of Philosophy</u> (New York: Macmillan Publishing Co., 1967), 82.

31. Titus et al., <u>Living Issues</u>, 132.

32. Abelson, "History of Ethics," 1000.

33. Titus, <u>Living Issues</u>, 104.

34. Ibid., 103.

35. Ibid., 122.

36. Ibid., 125-126.

37. Jose Ortega Y Gasset, <u>The Revolt of the Masses</u> (New York: W. W. Norton and Co., 1993), 125.

38. Ibid., 187.

39. Graham, <u>The Jesus Generation</u>, 13-23.

40. Grounds, <u>Revolution</u>, 107.

41. Ibid., 120.

42. Ibid., 122. Tom Skinner, <u>Words of Revolution</u>, 38-60.

43. See, for instance, Michael E. Marmura, ed., <u>Islamic Theology and Philosophy: Studies in Honor of George F. Hourani</u> (Albany: State University of New York Press, 1984), Franz Rosenthal, <u>The Muslim Conception of Freedom Prior to the 19th Century</u> (Leiden: E. J. Brill, 1960), and Duncan B. Macdonald, <u>Development of Muslim Theology, Jurisprudence and Constitutional Theory</u> (New York: Charles Scribner's Sons, 1903).

44. Robert Payne, <u>The History of Islam</u> (New York: Dorset Press, 1990), 29-86. See also Imam Muhammad Shirazi, <u>War, Peace and Non-Violence: An Islamic Perspective</u> (London: Fountain Books, 2001).

CHAPTER SIX: LEARNING FROM HISTORY – HEBREW, ENGLISH AND AMERICAN

1. Thomas Cahill, The Gifts of the Jews: How A Tribe of Desert Nomads Changed the Way Everyone Thinks and Feels (New York: Doubleday, 1998).
2. David Baron, Moses on Management: 50 Leadership Lessons From the Greatest Manager of All Time (New York: Simon and Schuster, 1999), xi.
3. David Biale, Power and Powerlessness in Jewish History (New York: Schocken Books, 1986), 15.
4. Oswald T. Allis, God Spake by Moses: An Exposition of the Pentateuch (Philadelphia, PA: Presbyterian and Reformed Publishing Co., 1951), 59.
5. Ibid., 54.
6. Cahill, The Gifts of the Jews, 271.
7. Ibid.
8. Allis, God Spake by Moses, 60.
9. Walther Kirchner, Western Civilization to 1500: Political, Cultural and Social History With Examinations (New York: Barnes and Noble Books, 1960), 290.
10. Cahill, 103.
11. Baron, xi-xiii.
12. H. H. Ben-Sasson, ed., A History of the Jewish People (Cambridge, MA: Harvard University Press, 2002), 42, G. E. Wright, "Book of Exodus," in George A. Butterick, The Interpreter's Dictionary of the Bible, 188-197, and Wright, "Route of Exodus," in George A. Butterick, The Interpreter's Dictionary of the Bible, 197 – 199.
13. Ben-Sasson, 43.
14. Paul Johnson, A History of the Jewish People (New York: Harper, 1988), 23.
15. Ibid., 25.
16. Ibid. See also S. J. DeVries, "Chronology of the OT," in Butterick, The Interpreter's Dictionary of the Bible, 584.
17. Johnson, 26.
18. Ibid.
19. Ibid.

20. Ibid., 26-27.
21. Ibid., 27.
22. Ibid.
23. Ibid., 23-24.
24. Ibid., 27.
25. Ibid.
26. Howard Fast, <u>The Jews: Story of A People</u> (New York: ibook Inc., 1968), 8.
27. Ibid., 7-8.
28. Ibid., 9-10.
29. Ibid., 16.
30. Ibid., (underlining added for emphasis).
31. Finis Jennings Dake, <u>Dake's Annotated Reference Bible</u> (Lawrenceville, GA" Dake Bible Sales, Inc., 1983), 72.
32. Ibid., 109 and 110.
33. Walter C. Kaiser, Jr., <u>Toward an Old Testament Theology</u> (Grand Rapids, MI: Zondervan, 1978), 103.
34. Paul R. House, <u>Old Testament Theology</u> (Downers Grove, IL: InterVarsity Press, 1998), 102 and 103.
35. On the origins of the English people, see Winston Churchill, <u>History of the English Speaking People: Birth of Britain, 55 B.C. to 1485</u> (New York: Barnes & Noble, 1995); Simon Schama, <u>A History of Britain, 2 vols</u>. (New York: Hyperion, 2001); and Stephen Oppenheimer, <u>The Origins of the British – A Genetic Detective Story: The Surprising Roots of the English, Irish, Scottish and Welsh</u> (New York: Carroll and Graf Publishers, 2006).
36. F. F. Bruce, <u>The Spreading Flame: The Rise and Progress of Christianity from John the Baptist to the Conversion of the English</u> (Exeter: The Paternoster Press, 1958), 353.
37. Philip Lee Ralph et al., <u>World Civilizations: Their History and Culture, vol. 2</u> (New York: W. W. Norton and Co., 1991), 97.
38. Eric Hobsbawm, <u>The Age of Revolution 1789-1848</u> (New York: Random House, 1996) and Herbert Aptheker, <u>The Nature of Democracy, Freedom, and Revolution</u> (New York: International Publishers, 1967), 74-128, (Chapters 5-8).
39. See Danny Danziger and John Gillingham, <u>1215: The Year of Magna Carta</u> (New York: Simon and Schuster, 2003) and

A. E. Dick Howard, <u>Magna Carta: Text and Commentary</u> (Charlottesville: University of Virginia Press, 1998).

40. Goldwin Smith, <u>A Constitutional and Legal History of England</u> (New York: Dorset Press, 1990), 122.

41. Ibid. See also M. M. Knappen, <u>Constitutional and Legal History of England</u> (Hamden, CT: Archon Books, 1964), 77-124.

42. Asa Briggs, <u>A Social History of England</u> (New York: The Viking Press, 1984), 52.

43. Ibid., 37.

44. Ibid.

45. Ibid., 43.

46. Ibid., 43 and 56.

47. Ibid., 59.

48. Ibid. See also 77-81 and Knappen, <u>Constitutional and Legal History of England</u>, 124-131. For an account of "the feudalization of the Crown," see pages 132-153. For an analysis of King John (1199-1216 A.D.), see Antonia Fraser, ed., <u>The Lives of the Kings and Queens of England</u> (New York: Alfred A. Knopf, 1975), 63-67.

49. See Danziger and Gillingham, 275-290.

50. See Mark Kishlansky, <u>A Monarchy Transformed: Britain 1603-1714</u> (New York: Penguin Books, 1996) and also Fraser, <u>The Lives of the Kings and Queens of England</u>, 221-231.

51 See Diane Purkiss, <u>The English Civil War: Papists, Gentlemen, Soldiers, and Witch-finders in the Birth of Modern Britain</u> (New York: Basic Books, 2006).

52. Geoffrey Robertson, <u>The Tyrannicide Brief: The Story of the Man Who Sent Charles I to the Scaffold</u> (New York: Pantheon Books, 2005).

53. Kishlansky, <u>A Monarchy Transformed</u>, 223.

54. Knappen, 233.

55. Ibid., 447-448; Ralph, <u>World Civilizations</u>, 2: 113-117. For recent works on the "Glorious Revolution" in England. See Michael Barone, <u>Our First Revolution: The Remarkable British Upheaval That Inspired America's Founding Fathers</u> (New York: Crown Publishers, 2007); Steven C. A. Pincus, <u>England's Glorious Revolution 1688-1689: A Brief History</u>

With Documents (New York: St. Martin's Press, 2005);
Edward Vallance, Glorious Revolution : 1688 – Britain's
Fight for Liberty (New York: Pegasus Books, 2007); and
Eveline Cruickshanks, Glorious Revolution: British History in
Perspective (New York: Palgrave Macmillan, 2007).

56. Barone, Our First Revolution, 200-233.

57. Ralph, World Civilizations, 2: 116.

58. The American War of Independence began on April 19, 1775
and ended in November 1782 when a preliminary treaty was
signed at Paris. A formal treaty was later signed on September 3,
1783.

59. Mary Beth Norton et al., A People and A Nation: A History
of the United States, vol., 1, 4th ed., (Boston, MA: Houghton
Mifflin Co., 1994), 128.

60. Gerald N. Grob and George Athan Billias, eds., Interpretations
of American History: Patterns and Perspectives, 5th ed. (New
York: The Free Press, 1987), 109-158.

61. Norton, A People and A Nation, 139-140.

62. M. Stanton Evans, The Theme is Freedom: Religion, Politics,
and the American Tradition (Washington, D.C: Regnery
Publishing Inc., 1994), 207.

63. Ibid.

64. Ibid.

65. Ibid., 208.

66. J. A. Leo Lemay, ed., The Oldest Revolutionary: Essays on
Benjamin Franklin (Philadelphia: University of Pennsylvania
Press, 1976.). See also Bernard Bailyn, The Ideological Origins
of the American Revolution, (Cambridge, MA: Harvard
University Press, 1967); Edmund S. Morgan, The Challenge of
the American Revolution (New York: W. W. Norton and Co.,
1976), 77; and Jack Fruchtman, Jr., Thomas Paine: Apostle of
Freedom (New York: Four Walls Eight Windows, 1994).

67. Norton, A People and A Nation, 123.

68. Ibid., 138.

69. Ibid., 155-158.

70. See Benjamin Quarles, The Negro in the American Revolution
(New York: W. W. Norton and Co., 1961).

71. Norton, A People and A Nation, 174-176.

72. See David Armitage, <u>The Declaration of Independence: A Global History</u> (Cambridge, MA: Harvard University Press, 2007) and Alfred W. Blumrosen and Ruth G. Blumrosen, <u>Slave Nation: How Slavery United the Colonies and Sparked the American Revolution</u> (Naperville, IL: Source Books, Inc., 2005).

73. Alan Gibson, <u>Interpreting the Founding: Guide to the Enduring Debates Over the Origins and Foundations of the American Republic</u> (Lawrence: University Press of Kansas, 2006).

74. This letter was discovered in the internet search and is now in the possession of this writer.

75. Adams, "The Meaning of the American Revolution," 1.

76. Ibid.

77. Ibid.

78. Ibid., 2.

79. Ibid.

80. Gordon S. Wood, <u>The American Revolution: A History</u> (New York: The Modern Library, 2003), 114-124. See also Edmund S. Morgan, <u>The Meaning of Independence</u> (Charlottesville: University of Virginia Press, 1976).

81. Edward Countryman, <u>The American Revolution</u> (New York: Hill and Wang, 2003), 208.

82. Ibid., 212 and 217.

83. Beard, <u>An Economic Interpretation of the Constitution</u>, 152ff.

84. Dan Lacy, <u>The Meaning of the American Revolution</u> (New York: The New American Library, 1964), 268-288.

85. Ibid., 268.

86. Ibid., 277.

87. Ibid., 280.

88. Henry Steele Commager, "Our Beginnings: A Lesson for Today," in Lawrence H. Leder, ed., <u>The Meaning of the American Revolution</u> (Chicago, IL: Quadrangle Books, 1969), 178-179.

89. Ibid., 185.

90. Ibid., 183.

91. Ibid., 185.

92. Ibid., 177.

93. Saul K. Padover, "Jefferson Still Survives," in Leder, ed., The Meaning of the American Revolution, 74.
94. Ibid.
95. Ibid., 76.
96. See Psalms 62: 11.

CHAPTER SEVEN: LEARNING FROM HISTORY – FRENCH, RUSSIAN AND CHINESE

1. Ralph, et al., World Civilization, 2: 185.
2. Ibid., 196, 292-298, and 299-303.
3. The literature on the origins and causes of the French Revolution is vast and extensive. See, for example, the following: Edmund Burke, Reflections on the Revolution in France (Mineola, NY: Dover Publications, 2006); Thomas Carlyle, The French Revolution: A History (New York: Random House, 2002); Christopher Hibbert, The Days of the French Revolution (New York: Perennial, 2002); and William Doyle, Origins of the French Revolution (New York: Oxford University Press, 1999).
4. Edmund Burke and Thomas Paine, Two Classics of the French Revolution (New York: Doubleday, 1989), 50.
5. Ibid., 21.
6. Ibid., 95.
7. Ibid., 140.
8. Ibid., 215.
9. Ibid., 219.
10. J. M. Thompson, Leaders of the French Revolution (New York: Basil Blackwell, Inc., 1988) has documented the contributions of eleven such leaders.
11. Ralph, World Civilizations, 2: 185-226.
12. See Georges Lefebvre, The Coming of the French Revolution, trans. R. R. Palmer (Princeton, NJ: Princeton University Press, 1989).
13. Ralph, World Civilizations, 2: 196.
14. Ibid.
15. Ibid., 201.
16. Ibid., 206. See also R. R. Palmer, Twelve Who Ruled: The

Year of the Terror in the French Revolution (Princeton, NJ: Princeton University Press, 1989, 1941).

17. Ralph, World Civilizations, 2: 207.
18. Ibid., 208-209.
19. Ibid., 209.
20. Ibid., 220.
21. Jacques Sole, Questions of the French Revolution: a Historical Overview (New York: Pantheon Books, 1989), 3.
22. Ibid.
23. Ibid., 22.
24. Ibid., 62.
25. Ibid., 72.
26. Renee Waldinger, Philip Dawson, and Isser Woloch, eds., The French Revolution and the Meaning of Citizenship (Westport, CT: Greenwood Publishing Group, 1993).
27. See Gutierrez, The Power of the Poor in History and Iliffe, The African Poor: A History, both already cited.
28. See W. O. Maloba, African Women in Revolution (Trenton, NJ: Africa World Press, 2007), and Ike Okonta, When Citizens Revolt: Nigerian Elites, Big Oil and the Ogoni Struggle For Self-Determination (Trenton, NJ: Africa World Press, 2008).
29. George Vernadsky, The Origins of Russia (Oxford: Clarendon Press, 1959), 277.
30. See Raymond E. Zickel, ed., Soviet Union: A Country Study (Washington, D.C: Government Printing Office, 1991).
31. See Encyclopedia Britannica, vol. 10 (Full citation needed).
32. For a fuller biography of Nicholas II, see Robert D. Warth, Nicholas II: The Life and Reign of Russia's Last Monarch (Westport, CT: Praeger, 1997).
33. Ralph, World Civilizations, 2: 441.
34. Ibid., 442-443.
35. Ibid., 516.
36. For a scholarly analysis of the life and role of Lenin in Russian history, see Corinne J. Naden, Lenin (San Diego, CA: Lucent Books, 2004), Harold Shukman, Lenin and the Russian Revolution (Hoboken, NJ: Wiley-Blackwell, 1994), and Georges Haupt, Makers of the Russian Revolution: Biographies of Bolshevik Leaders (Ithaca, NY: Cornell University Press, 1974).

See also Bertram D. Wolfe, <u>Three Who Made A Revolution: A Biographical History of Lenin, Trotsky, and Stalin</u> (New York: Cooper Square Press, 2001).

37. See Robert Service, <u>A History of Modern Russia from Nicholas II to Vladimir Putin</u> (Cambridge, MA: Harvard University Press, , 2003, 1997) and Edvard Radzinsky, <u>The Last Tsar: The Life and Death of Nicholas II</u> (New York: Anchor Books, 1993).

38. Robert Service, <u>Lenin: A Biography</u> (Cambridge, MA: Harvard University Press, 2000); Paul Gabel, <u>And God Created Lenin: Marxism vs. Religion in Russia, 1917-1929</u> (Amherst, NY: Prometheus Books, 2005) and Richard Pipes, <u>Russia Under the Bolshevik Regime</u> (New York: Vintage Books, 1995).

39. Ralph, <u>World Civilizations</u>, 2: 537.

40. Ibid., 2: 540. See also Leon Trotsky, <u>The History of the Russian Revolution</u> (New York: Pathfinder, 2001, 1980), and his other book, <u>The Revolution Betrayed</u> (Mineola, New York: Dover Publications, 2004).

41. Ralph, <u>World Civilizations</u>, 2: 541.

42. Ibid., 2: 540.

43. Ibid. For scholarly treatments of Stalin, see Robert Conquest, <u>Stalin: Breaker of Nations</u> (New York: Penguin, 1991); Robert Service, <u>Stalin: A Biography</u> (Cambridge, MA: Harvard University Press, 2004); and Edvard Radzinsky, <u>Stalin: The First In-depth Biography Based on Explosive New Documents from Russia's Archives</u> (New York: Anchor Books, 1997). See also Robert Vincent Daniels, <u>The Stalin Revolution: Foundations of the Totalitarian Era </u>(Lexington, MA: D. C. Heath and Co., 1990).

44. John M. Thompson, <u>Revolutionary Russia, 1917</u> (New York: Charles Scribner's Sons, 1981), 18. See also pp. 16-17.

45. Ibid., 19.

46. Ibid., 21.

47. Ibid.

48. Ibid., 9-16.

49. Ibid., 94.

50. Ibid., 126.

51. Ibid., 156-177.

52. Ibid., 177. See also Sheila Fitzpatrick, The Russian Revolution (New York: Oxford University Press, 1994), 40-67.
53. Fitzpatrick, 70 and Thompson, Revolutionary Russia, 181-183.
54. Fitzpatrick, 74.
55. Orlando Figes, A People 's Tragedy: The Russian Revolution 1891-1924 (New York: Penguin, 1996), 307-353 and see also Robert Conquest, The Great Terror: A Reassessment (New York: Oxford University Press, 1990).
56. See John Reed, Ten Days That Shook the World (New York: Penguin, 1977, 1919); Donald Rayfield, Stalin and His Hangmen: The Tyrant and Those Who Killed for Him (New York: Random House, 2004); and Joshua Rubenstein and Vladimir P. Naumou, eds., Stalin's Secret Pogrom: The Post-War Inquisition of the Jewish Anti-Fascist Committee (New Haven, CT: Yale University Press, 2005).
    Some scholars believe that the number killed, banished, or imprisoned under Stalin was only about nine million people. But what difference does it make? See Ralph, World Civilizations, 2: 544. The Reverend D. James Kennedy of Fort Lauderdale, Florida, gave the number killed as ten million.
57. Thompson, Revolutionary Russia, 183-188.
58. Ibid., 183.
59. Ibid., 188.
60. Fitzpatrick, The Russian Revolution, 170.
61. Ibid.
62. Ibid., 171.
63. Nicolas Berdyaev, The Origin of Russian Communism (Ann Arbor: The University of Michigan Press, 1999), 117. See also Eric Hobsbawn, On History (New York: The New Press, 1997), 241-252.
64. Figes, A People's Tragedy, 352-353. See also Maxim Matusevich, ed., Africa in Russia, Russia in Africa: Three Centuries of Encounters (Trenton, NJ: Africa World Press, 2007) and Allison Blakely, Russia and the Negro: Blacks in Russian History and Thought (Washington, D.C: Howard University Press, 1986).
65. See Patrice Hill, "China Becomes the Growth Engine: U. S.

Dislodged As World's Pace-setter," <u>The Washington Times</u> (July 26, 2007), front-page.

66. Bamber Gascoigne, <u>The Dynasties of China: A History</u> (New York: Caroll and Graf Publishers, 2005).

67. There are many historical accounts of China. See the following: J. A. G. Roberts, <u>The Complete History of China</u> (Phoenix Hill, Britain: Sutton Publishing, 2006); Edward L. Shaughnessy, ed., <u>China, Empire and Civilization</u> (New York: Oxford University Press, 2005); W. Scott Morton and Charlton M. Lewis, <u>China: Its History and Culture</u> (New York: McGraw Hill, 2005); Jeremiah Curtin, <u>The Mongols: A History</u> (Cambridge, MA: Da Capo Press, 2003); John King Fairbank and Merle Goldman, <u>China: A New History</u> (Cambridge, MA: Harvard University Press, 1998); Mark Edward Lewis, <u>The Early Chinese Empires Qin and Han</u> (Cambridge, MA: Harvard University Press, 2007); Charles Benn, <u>China's Golden Age: Everyday Life in the Tang Dynasty</u> (New York: Oxford University Press, 2002); Jonathan D. Spence, <u>Emperor of China: Self-Portrait of K'ang-hsi</u> (New York: Vintage Books, 1988) and Harry G. Gelber, <u>The Dragon and the Foreign Devils: China and the World, 1100 B. C. to the Present</u> (New York: Walker and Co., 2007).

68. On Chinese Revolutions, see John King Fairbank, <u>The Great Chinese Revolution 1800-1985</u> (New York: Harper and Row, 1987); Rana Mitter, <u>A Bitter Revolution: China's Struggle With the Modern World</u> (New York: Oxford University Press, 2005) and Roderick Macfarquhar and Michael Schoehals, <u>Mao's Last Revolution</u> (Cambridge, MA: Harvard University Press, 2006).

69. See Charles O. Hucker, <u>China's Imperial Past: An Introduction to Chinese History and Culture</u> (Stanford, CA: Stanford University Press, 1975).

70. Jung Chang and Jon Halliday, <u>Mao: The Unknown Story</u> (New York: Random House, 2006). See also Fiona Macdonald, <u>Mao Zedong: The Rebel Who Led A Revolution</u> (Washington, D. C: National Geographic, 2007); Ann Malaspina, <u>The Chinese Revolution and Mao Zedong in World History</u> (Berkeley Heights, NJ: Enslow Publishers, 2004); Yu Siao, <u>Mao-Tse-tung and I Were Beggars</u> (New York: Collier Books, 1973); and Anne

Fremantle, ed., <u>Mao Tse-tung: An Anthology of His Writings</u> (New York: The New American Library, 1962).

71. Chang and Halliday, <u>Mao</u>, 4-5. See also Philip Short, <u>Mao: A Life</u> (New York: Henry Holt and Co., 2001); Li-Zhisui, <u>The Private Life of Chairman Mao</u> (New York: Random House, 1994); Maurice Meisner, <u>Mao-Zedong: A Political and Intellectual Portrait</u> (Malden, MA: Polity Press, 2007); Jonathan Spence, <u>Mao-Zedong: A Penguin Life</u> (New York: Penguin, 1999); and Michael Lynch, <u>Mao</u> (London: Routledge, 2004).

72. Chang and Halliday, <u>Mao</u>, 6.

73. Ibid., 10-11.

74. Ibid., 11.

75. See Charles Benn, <u>China's Golden Age</u> (2002).

76. Chang and Halliday, <u>Mao</u>, 12.

77. Ibid., 13.

78. Ibid.

79. Ibid.

80. Ibid., 14.

81. Ibid., 15.

82. Ralph, <u>World Civilizations</u>, 2: 723-724.

83. Ibid., 730.

84. Ibid., 729 and 731.

85. Ibid., 732.

86. Ibid.

87. Ibid.

88. Ibid.

89. Ibid., 733.

90. Ibid.

91. Ibid., 736.

92. Ibid., 737. See also C. M. Wilbur, ed., <u>Mao Tse-tung in the Scales of History: A Preliminary Assessment</u> (New York: Cambridge University Press, 1977).

93. Chang and Halliday, Mao, 616.

94. Ibid., 3. See also H. R. Isaacs, <u>The Tragedy of the Chinese Revolution</u> (Stanford, CA: Stanford University Press, 1961).

95. Kennedy, <u>What If Jesus Had Never Been Born,?</u> 2: 235 and 236.

96. Chang and Halliday, <u>Mao</u>, 475.

Chapter Eight: Decolonization

1. Walter Rodney, <u>How Europe Underdeveloped Africa</u> (Washington, D.C: Howard University Press, 1982) and W. E. B. Du Bois, <u>The World and Africa: An Inquiry Into the Part Which Africa Has Played in World History</u> (New York: International Publishers, 1987), 44-80, "The Rape of Africa."

2. Norman R. Bennett, <u>Africa and Europe from Roman Times to National Independence</u> (New York: Africana Publishing Co., 1984), 178.

3. See Leonard Thompson, <u>A History of South Africa</u> (New Haven, CT: Yale University Press, 2000).

4. See D. K. Fieldhouse, <u>Black Africa, 1945-1980: Economic Decolonization and Arrested Development</u> (London: Allen and Unwin, 1986); <u>Colonialism, 1870-1945: An Introduction</u> (New York: St. Martin's Press, 1981); L. H. Gann and Peter Duignan, eds., <u>Colonialism in Africa, 1870-1960, vol. 2</u> (London: Cambridge University Press, 1970).

5. Adebayo Adedeji, "Comparative Strategies of Economic Decolonization in Africa," in Ali A. Mazrui, ed., <u>General History of Africa, vol., 8</u> (Berkeley: University of California Press, 1999), 393, "footnote.

6. See James D. Le Sueur, ed., <u>The Decolonization Reader</u> (New York: Routledge, 2003), 2. See also Linda T. Smith, <u>Decolonizing Methodologies: Research and Indigenous Peoples</u> (London: Zed Books, 1999) and John Darwin, <u>Britain and Decolonization: The Retreat from Empire in the Post-War World</u> (New York: Palgrave Macmillan, 1988).

7. This definition is taken from www.socialpolicy.ca/d.htm. on the internet. See also Lilyan Kesteloot, <u>Intellectual Origins of the African Revolution</u> (Washington, D. C: Black Orpheus Press, 1972).

8. Prasenjit Duara, <u>Decolonization: Perspectives from Now and Then</u> (New York: Routledge, 2003), 2, and M. Chamberlain, <u>Decolonization: The Fall of the European Empires</u> (Oxford: University Press, 1999).

9. Crawford Young, "Decolonization in Africa," in Gann and Duignan, eds., <u>Colonialism in Africa</u>, 2: 450-502.

10. Frantz Fanon, <u>The Wretched of the Earth</u>, 37, and Mandisi Majavu, "Fanon Revisited," an article posted on the internet site: www.http//blog.zmag.org. dated February 13, 2005.

11. Jeremi Suri, <u>Power and Protest: Global Revolution and the Rise of Détente</u> (Cambridge, MA: Harvard University Press, 2003), inside front-cover jacket.

12. See the following: Robert I Rotberg and Ali A. Mazrui, eds., <u>Power and Protest in Black Africa</u> (New York: Oxford University Press, 1970); A Adu Boahen, <u>African Perspectives on Colonialism</u> (Baltimore, MD: The Johns Hopkins University Press, 1987), 34-57; Michael Crowder, ed., <u>West African Resistance: The Military Response to Colonial Occupation</u> (New York: Africana Publishing Co., 1972); and David L. Lewis, <u>The Race to Fashoda: Colonialism and African Resistance</u> (New York: Henry Holt and Co., 1987).

13. Emma S. Etuk, <u>Destiny is Not A Matter of Chance</u>, 121-133.

14. Etuk, <u>Listen Africans</u>, 19-20.

15. Ibid., 19.

16. Boahen, <u>African Perspectives</u>, 94-112.

17. See "Social Capital Definitions," in http://www.gnudung.com/literature/definition/html.

18. James S. Coleman, <u>Nigeria: Background to Nationalism</u> (Berkeley: University of California Press, 1958); Hugh H. and Mabel M. Smythe, <u>The New Nigerian Elite</u> (Stanford, CA: Stanford University Press, 1960); and Richard L. Sklar, <u>Nigerian Political Parties</u> (Princeton, NJ: Princeton University Press, 1963). See also Thomas Hodgkin, <u>Nationalism in Colonial Africa</u> (New York: New York University Press, 1957) and Hans Kohn and Wallace Sokolsky, <u>African Nationalism in the Twentieth Century</u> (Princeton, NJ: D. Van Nostrand Co., 1965).

19. Raph Uwachue, <u>Makers of Modern Africa: Profiles in History</u> (London: Africa Books Ltd., 1991), iv.

Chapter Nine: Preparing Ourselves

1. Emma S. Etuk, <u>The Indispensable Visionary: Turning Your Dreams into Realities</u> (Washington, D. C: Emida International Publishers, 2006), 118-120.
2. Ibid., 127.
3. Ibid., 128.
4. Alfred Lord Tennyson cited in Etuk, <u>Recipe for Success: The 21 Indispensable Things That Can Help You Succeed in Life</u> (Washington, D. C: Emida International Publishers, 2004), 98.
5. S. J. De Vries, "Chronology of the OT," cited in George A. Buttrick, ed., <u>The Interpreter's Dictionary of the Bible, vol. 1</u> (Nashville, TN: Abingdon Press, 1962), 580-599. Some experts date the Exodus as occurring around 1290 B.C. or 1280 B.C.
6. According to the Bible (Judges 8: 28), it is apparent that Gideon ruled Israel for about forty years.

Chapter Ten: Conclusion

1. John F. Kennedy cited in Bartlett, <u>Familiar Quotations</u>, 891.

SELECTED BIBLIOGRAPHY

Abrahamov, Binyamin, ed. Islamic Theology: Traditionalism and Rationalism. Edinburgh: Edinburgh University Press, 1988.

Adedeji, Adebayo. "Com-parative Strategies of Economic Decolonization in Africa," in Mazrui, Ali A., ed. General History of Africa, vol. 8, Berkeley: University of California Press, 1999.

Allis, Oswald T. God Spake By Moses: An Exposition of the Pentateuch. Philadelphia, PA: Presbyterian and Reformed Publishing Co., 1951.

Aptheker, Herbert. The Nature of Democracy, Freedom, and Revolution. New York: International Publishers, 1967.

Arendt, Hannah. On Revolution. New York: Penguin Books, 1965.

_____ The Origins of Totalitarianism. New York: Schoken Books, 1976.

Armitage, David. The Declaration of Independence: A Global History. Cambridge, MA: Harvard University Press, 2007.

Ayisi, Eric O. An Introduction to the Study of African Culture. London: Heinemann, 1972.

Aya, Roderick. National Liberation: Revolution in the Third World. New York: The Free Press, 1971.

Ayittey, George B. N. Indigenous African Institutions. Ardsley-on-Hudson, New York: Transnational Publishers, 1991.

Bailyn, Bernard. The Ideological Origins of the American Revolution. Cambridge, MA: Harvard University Press, 1967.

Baron, David. <u>Moses on Management: 50 Leadership Lessons from the Greatest Manager of All Time</u>. New York: Simon and Schuster, 1999.

Barone, Michael. <u>Our First Revolution: The Remarkable British Upheaval that Inspired America's Founding Fathers</u>. New York: Crown Publishers, 2007.

Bartlett, John. <u>Familiar Quotations</u>. Boston, MA: Little, Brown and Co., 1980.

Bassett, Thomas J. <u>The Peasant Cotton Revolution in West Africa, Cote d'Ivoire, 1880-1995</u>. New York: Cambridge University Press, 2001.

Beard, Charles A. <u>An Economic Interpretation of the Constitution of the United States</u>. New York: The Free Press, 1913.

Benn, Charles. <u>China's Golden Age: Everyday Life in the Tang Dynasty</u>. New York: Oxford University Press, 2002.

Bennett, Norman R. <u>Africa and Europe from Roman Times to National Independence</u>. New York: Africana Publishing Co., 1984.

Ben-Sasson, H. H., ed. <u>A History of the Jewish People.</u> Cambridge, MA: Harvard University Press, 2002.

Berdyaev, Nicolas. <u>The Origin of Russian Communism</u>. Ann Arbor: The University of Michigan Press, 1999.

Biale, David. <u>Power and Powerlessness in Jewish History</u>. New York: Schoken Books, 1986.

Blakely, Allison. <u>Russia and the Negro: Blacks in Russian History and Thought</u>. Washington, D.C.: Howard University Press, 1986.

Blumrosen, Alfred W. and Blumrosen, Ruth G. <u>Slave Nation: How Slavery United the Colonies and Sparked the American Revolution</u>. Naperville, IL: Source Books, Inc., 2005.

Boahen, A. Adu. <u>African Perspectives on Colonialism</u>. Baltimore, MD: The Johns Hopkins University Press, 1987.

Bok, Francis. <u>Escape from Slavery: The True Story of My Ten Years</u>

in Captivity - and My Journey to Freedom in America. New York: St. Martin's Press, 2003.

Bolton, Giles. Africa Doesn't Matter: How the West Has Failed the Poorest Continent and What We Can Do About It. New York: Arcabe Publishing, 2007.

Briggs, Asa. A Social History of England. New York: The Viking Press, 1984.

Brinton, Crane. The Anatomy of Revolution. New York: Random House, 1965.

Bruce, F. F. The Spreading Flame: The Rise and Progress of Christianity from John the Baptist to the Conversion of the English. Exeter: The Paternoster Press, 1958.

Burke, Edmund. Reflections on the Revolution in France. Mineola, New York: Dover Publications, 2006.

_____ and Paine, Thomas. Two Classics of the French Revolution. New York: 1989.

Buttrick, George Arthur, ed. The Interpreter's Dictionary of the Bible, vol. 4. Nashville, TN: Abingdon Press, 2000.

Canhill, Thomas. The Gifts of the Jews: How a tribe of Desert Nomads Changed the Way Everyone Thinks and Feels. New York: Doubleday, 1998.

Carlyle, Thomas. The French Revolution: A History. New York: Random House, 2002.

Carroll, Warren H. The Revolution Against Christendom: A History of Christendom, vol. 5. Wilmington, DE: ISI Books, 2006.

Chamberlain, M. Decolonization: The Fall of the European Empires. Oxford: University Press, 1999.

Chang, Jung and Halliday, Jon. Mao: The Unknown Story. New York: Anchor Books, 2006.

Cheru, Fantu. The Silent Revolution in Africa: Debt, Development and Democracy. London: Zed Books Ltd., 1993.

Churchill, Wiston. History of the English Speaking People: Birth of Britain, 55 B.C. to 1485. New York: Barnes and Noble, 1995.

Claiborne, Shane. The Irresistible Revolution: Living As An Ordinary Radical. Grand Rapids, MI: Zondervan, 2006.

Clarke, John Henrik. Who Betrayed the African World Revolution? and other Speeches. Chicago, IL: Third World Press, 1994.

_____ My Life in Search of Africa. Chicago, IL: Third World Press, 1989.

Coleman, James S. Nigeria: Background to Nationalism. Berkeley: University of California Press, 1958.

Cone, James H. God of the Oppressed. Mineapolis, MN: The Seabury Press, 1975.

Conquest, Robert. Stalin: Breaker of Nations. New York: Penguin, 1991.

_____ The Great Terror: A Reassessment. New York: Oxford University Press, 1990.

Crowther, Michael, ed. West African Resistance: The Military Response to Colonial Occupation. New York: Africana Publishing Co., 1972.

Cruickshanks, Eveliner. Glorious Revolution: British History in Perspective. New York: Palgrave Macmillan, 2007.

Curtin, Jeremiah. The Mongols: A History. Cambridge, MA: Da Capo Press, 2003.

Dake, Finis Jennings. Dake's Annotated Reference Bible. Lawrenceville, GA: Dake Bible Sales, Inc., 1983.

Daniels, Robert Vincent. The Stalin Revolution: Foundations of the Totalitarian Era. Lexington, MA: D.C. Heath and Co., 1990.

Danziger, Danny and Gillingham, John. 1215: The Year of Magna Carter. New York: Simon and Schuster, 2003.

Darwin, John. Britain and Decolonization: The Retreat from Empire in the Post-War World. New York: Palgrave Macmillan, 1988.

Dinerman, Alice. Revolution, Counter-Revolution and Revisionism in Post-Colonial Africa: The Case of Mozambique, 1975-1994. New York: Routledge, 2006.

Doyle, William. <u>Origins of the French Revolution</u>. New York: Oxford University Press, 1999.

Duara, Prasenjit. <u>Decolonization: Perspectives from Now and Then</u>. New York: Routledge, 2003.

Du Bois, W. E. B. <u>The World and Africa: An Inquiry into the Part Which Africa Has Played in World History</u>. New York: International Publishers, 1987.

Durant, Will and Ariel. <u>Rousseau and Revolution</u>, vol. 10. New York: Simon and Schuster, 1967.

Edwards, Paul, ed. <u>The Encyclopedia of Philosophy</u>. New York: Macmillan Publishing Co., 1967.

Esposito, John. <u>The Islamic Threat: Myth or Reality?</u> New York: Oxford University Press, 1992.

Etuk, Emma S. <u>Destiny is Not A Matter of Chance: Essays in Reflection and Contemplation on the Destiny of Blacks</u>. New York: Peter Lang, 1989.

_____ <u>Listen Africans: Freedom is Under Fire</u>. Washington, D.C.: Emida International Publishers, 2002.

_____ <u>The Indispensable Visionary: Turning Your Dreams Into Realities</u>. Washington, D.C.: Emida International Publishers, 2006.

_____ <u>NEVER AGAIN: Africa's Last Stand</u>. Bloomington, IN: iuniverse, Inc., 2008.

_____ <u>A SPLENDID ECSTASY: The Trials, Thrills and Joys of Authorship</u>. Bloomington, IN: Authorhouse, Inc., 2010.

_____ <u>The Audacity of Faith: The Relevance of Faith to Success</u>. Bloomington, IN: iuniverse, Inc., 2010.

Evans, M. Stanton. <u>The Theme is Freedom: Religion, Politics, and the American Tradition</u>. Washington, D.C.: Regnery Publishing Inc., 1994.

Fairbank, John King. <u>The Great Chinese Revolution 1800-1985</u>. New York: Harper and Row, 1986.

_____ and Goldman, Merle. China: A New History. Cambridge, MA: Harvard University Press, 1998.

Fanon, Frantz. The Wretched of the Earth. New York: Grove Press, 1963.

_____ Toward the African Revolution: Political Essays. New York: Grove Press, 1964.

Fast, Howard. The Jews: Story of a People. New York: ibook, Inc., 1968.

Fieldhouse, D.K. Black Africa, 1945-80: Economic Decolonization and Arrested Development. London: Allen and Unwin, 1986.

_____ Colonialism, 1870-1945: An Introduction. New York: St. Martin's Press, 1981.

Figes, Orlando. A People's Tragedy: The Russian Revolution 1891-1924. New York: Penguin, 1996.

Fischer, Louise. Gandhi: His Life and Message for the World. New York: New American Library, 1982.

Fisher, Humphrey J. Slavery in the History of Muslim Black Africa. Washington Square, New York: New York University Press, 2001.

Fitzpatrick, Sheila. The Russian Revolution. New York: Oxford University Press, 1994.

Franklin, Benjamin. The Autobiography of Benjamin Franklin. Mineola, New York: Dover Publications, Inc., 1996.

Fraser, Antonia, ed. The Lives of the Kings and Queens of England. New York: Afred A. Knopf, 1975.

Fruchtman, Jack, Jr. Thomas Paine: Apostle of Freedom. New York: Four Walls Eight Windows, 1994.

Gabel, Paul. And God Created Lenin: Marxism vs. Religion in Russia 1917-1929. Amherst, New York: Prometheus Books, 2005.

Gann, L. H. and Duignan, Peter, eds. Colonialism in Africa, 1870-1960, vol. 2. London: Cambridge University Press, 1970.

Garrow, David J. Bearing the Cross: Martin Luther King, Jr., and the Southern Christian Leadership Conference. New York: Random House, 1988.

Gascoigne, Bamber. The Dynasties of China: A History. New York: Carroll and Graf, Publishers, 2005.

Gasset, Jose Ortega. The Revolt of the Masses. New York: W. W. Norton and Co., 1993.

Gelber, Harry G. The Dragon and the Foreign Devils: China and the World, 1100 B.C. to the Present. New York: Walker and Co., 2007.

Ghazvinian, John. Untapped: The Scramble for Africa's Oil. Orlando, FL: Harcourt, Inc., 2007.

Gibson, Alan. Interpreting the Founding: Guide to the Enduring Debates Over the Origins and Foundations of the American Republic. Lawrence: University Press of Kansas, 2006.

Goldsworthy, Adrian. How Rome Fell: Death of a Superpower. New Haven, CT: Yale University Press, 2009.

Graham, Billy. The Jesus Generation. Grand Rapids, MI: Zondervan Publishing House, 1971.

Grob, Gerald N. and Billias, George Athan, eds. Interpretations of American History: Patterns and Perspectives, 2 vols. New York: The Free Press, 1987.

Grounds, Vernon C. Revolution and the Christian Faith. Philadelphia, PA: J. B. Lippincott Co., 1971.

Gutierrez, Gustavo. The Power of the Poor in History. Maryknoll, New York: Orbis Books, 1984.

Harris, Joseph E., ed. Global Dimensions of the African Diaspora. Washington, D.C.: Howard University Press, 1982.

_____ The African Presence in Asia: Consequences of the East African Slave Trade. Evanston, IL: Northwestern University Press, 1971.

Hartman, Robert H., ed. Poverty and Economic Justice: A Philosophical Approach. New York: Paulist Press, 1984.

Hashmi, Sohail H., ed. Islamic Political Ethics: Civil Society,

Pluralism, and Conflict. Princeton, NJ: Princeton University Press, 2002.

Haupt, Georges. Makers of the Russian Revolution: Biographies of Bolshevik Leaders. Ithaca, New York: Cornell University Press, 1974.

Herzog, Chaim and Gichon, Mordechai. Battles of the Bible: A Military History of Ancient Israel. New York: Barnes and Noble, 2006.

Hibbert, Christopher. The Days of the French Revolution. New York: Perennial, 2000.

Hobsbawn, Eric. On History. New York: The New Press, 1997.

_____ The Age of Revolution 1789-1848. New York: Random House, 1996.

Hodgkin, Thomas. Nationalism in Colonial Africa. New York: New York University Press, 1957.

House, Paul R. Old Testament Theology. Downer's Grove, IL: Intervarsity Press, 1998.

Howard, A. E. Dick. Magna Carter: Text and Commentary. Charlottesville: University of Virginia Press, 1998.

Hucker, Charles O. China's Imperial Past: An Introduction to Chinese History and Culture. Stanford, CA: Stanford University Press, 1975.

Hutchinson, Alan. China's African Revolution. Boulder, CO: Westview Press, 1976.

Iliffe, John. The African Poor: A History. New York: Cambridge University Press, 1987.

James, C. L. R. A History of Pan-African Revolt. n.p.: Drum and Spear Press, 1961.

Jameson, John Franklin. American Revolution Considered As a Social Movement. Princeton, NJ: Princeton University Press, 1968.

Johnson, Paul. A History of the Jewish People. New York: Harper, 1988.

Kaiser, Walter C., Jr. <u>Toward An Old Testament Theology</u>. Grand Rapids, MI: Zondervan, 1978.

Kanza, Thomas. <u>Africa Must Change: An African Manifesto</u>. Cambridge, MA: Schenkman Publishing Co., 1978.

Karsh, Effraim. <u>Islamic Imperialism: A History</u>. New Haven, CT: Yale University Press, 2006.

Kennedy, D. James and Newcombe, Jerry. <u>What if Jesus Had Never Been Born? The Positive Impact of Christianity in History</u>. Nashville, TN: Thomas Nelson Publishers, 1994.

Kesteloot, Lilyan. <u>Intellectual Origins of the African Revolution</u>. Washington, D.C.: Black Orpheus Press, 1972.

Khadduri, Majid. <u>The Islamic Conception of Justice</u>. Washington, D.C.: The Johns Hopkins University Press, 1984.

King, Martin Luther, Jr. <u>Why We Can't Wait</u>. New York: The New American Library, 1963.

Kinsella, David and Carr, Craig L., ed. <u>The Morality of War: A Reader</u>. Boulder, CO: Lynne Rienner Publishers, 2007.

Kirchner, Walther. <u>Western Civilization to 1500: Political, Cultural and Social History With Examinations</u>. New York: Barnes and Noble Books, 1960.

Kishlansky, Mark. <u>A Monarchy Transformed: Britain 1603-1714</u>. New York: Penguin Books, 1996.

Knappen, M. M. <u>Constitutional and Legal History of England</u>. Hamden, CT: Archon Books, 1964.

Kohn, Hans and Sokolsky, Wallace. <u>African Nationalism in the Twentieth Century</u>. Princeton, NJ: D. Van Nostrand Co., 1965.

Kurt, Laura. <u>An African Education: The Social Revolution in Tanzania</u>. Brooklyn, New York: Pageant Poseidon Ltd., 1972.

Lacy, Dan. <u>The Meaning of the American Revolution</u>. New York: The New American Library, 1964.

Laski, Harold J. <u>The Communist Manifesto</u>. New York: New American Library, 1967.

Leder, Lawrence H., ed. <u>The Meaning of the American Revolution</u>. Chicago, IL: Quadrangle Books, 1969.

Lefebvre, Georges. <u>The Coming of the French Revolution</u>. Princeton, NJ: Princeton University Press, 1989.

Lemay, J. A. Leo, ed. <u>The Oldest Revolutionary: Essays on Benjamin Franklin</u>. Philadelphia, PA: University of Pennsylvania Press, 1976.

Le Sueur, James D., ed. <u>The Decolonization Reader</u>. New York: Routledge, 2003.

Lewis, Bernard. <u>Race and Slavery in the Middle East: An Historical Enquiry</u>. New York: Oxford University Press, 1990.

Lewis, David L. <u>The Race to Fashoda: Colonialism and African Resistance</u>. New York: Henry Holt and Co., 1987.

Lewis, Mark Edward. <u>The Early Chinese Empires Qin and Han</u>. Cambridge, MA: Harvard University Press, 2007.

Littell, Robert. <u>The Revolutionist</u>. New York: Penguin, 2009.

Li-Zhisui. <u>The Private Life of Chairman Mao</u>. New York: Random House, 1994.

Lofchie, Michael. <u>Zanzibar: Background to Revolution</u>. Princeton, NJ: Princeton University Press, 1965.

Lowy, Michael. <u>The theory of Revolution in the Young Marx</u>. Chicago, IL: Haymarket Books, 2003.

Lynch, Michael L. <u>Mao</u>. London: Routledge, 2004.

Maathai, Wangari. <u>The Challenge for Africa</u>. New York: Pantheon Books, 2009.

Macfarquhar, Roderick and Schoenhals, Michael. <u>Mao's Last Revolution</u>. Cambridge, MA: The Belknap Press, 2006.

Maloba, W. O. <u>African Women in Revolution</u>. Trenton, NJ: Africa World Press, 2007.

Marmura, Michael E., ed. <u>Islamic Theology and Philosophy: Studies in honor of George F. Hourani</u>. Albany: State University of New York Press, 1984.

Matusevich, Maxim., ed. <u>Africa in Russia, Russia in Africa: Three Centuries of Encounter</u>. Trenton, NJ: Africa World Press, 2007.

Mbiti, John S. <u>African Religions and Philosophy</u>. Garden City, NY: Doubleday and Co., 1970.

Macdonald, Duncan B. <u>Development of Muslim Theology, Jurisprudence and Constitutional Theory</u>. New York: Charles Scribner's Sons, 1903.

McDonald, Forrest. <u>Novus Ordo Seclorum: The Intellectual Origins of the Constitution</u>. Lawrence: University of Kansas, 1985.

McLellan, David., ed. <u>Karl Marx: Selected Writings</u>. Oxford: Oxford University Press, 1977.

Mead, Walter Russell. <u>God and Gold: Britain, America, and the Making of the Modern World</u>. New York: Vintage Books, 2007.

Meisner, Maurice. <u>Mao Zedong: A Political and Intellectual Portrait</u>. Malden, MA: Polity Press, 2007.

Mitter, Rana. <u>A Bitter Revolution: China's Struggle With the Modern World</u>. Oxford: Oxford University Press, 2005.

_____ <u>Selected Works of Mao Tse-tung</u>, vol. 1. Beijing: n.p., 1975.

Moore, Barrington, Jr. <u>Reflections on the Causes of Human Misery and Upon Certain Proposals to Eliminate Them</u>. Boston, MA: Beacon Press, 1969.

Morgan, Edmund S. <u>The Challenge of the American Revolution</u>. New York: W. W. Norton and Co., 1976.

_____ <u>The Meaning of Independence</u>. Charlottesville: University of Virginia Press, 1976.

Morton, W. Scott, and Lewis, Charlton M. <u>China: Its History and Culture</u>. New York: McGraw Hill, 2005.

Moses, Wilson Jeremiah. <u>The Golden Age of Black Nationalism 1850-1925</u>. New York: Oxford University Press, 1978.

Naden, Corinne J. <u>Lenin</u>. San Diego, CA: Lucent Books, 2004.

Nazer, Mende. <u>Slave: My True Story</u>. New York: Public Affairs, 2003.

Nielson, Kai. Ethics Without God. Amherst, New York: Prometheus Books, 1990.

Norton, Mary Beth, et al. A People and A Nation: A History of the United States, 2 vols. Boston, MA: Houghton Mifflin Co., 1994.

Okonta, Ike. When Citizens Revolt: Nigerian Elites, Big Oil, and the Ogoni Struggle for Self-Determination. Trenton, NJ: Africa World Press, 2008.

Oppenheimer, Stephen. The Origins of the British — A Genetic Detective Story: The Surprising Roots of the English, Irish, Scotish and Welsh. New York: Carroll and Graf Publishers, 2006.

Padover, Saul K. Karl Marx: An Intimate Biography. New York: New American Library, 1980.

Palmer, R. R. Twelve Who Ruled: The Year of the Terror in the French Revolution. Princeton, NJ: Princeton University Press, 1989.

Paul, Ron. The Revolution: A Manifesto. New York: Grand Central Publishing, 2008.

Payne, Robert. The History of Islam. New York: Dorset Press, 1990.

Perkins, John. A Quiet Revolution: The Christian Response to Human Need ... A Strategy for Today. Waco, TX: Word Books, 1976.

Pincus, Steven C. A. England's Glorious Revolution 1688-1689: A Brief History With Documents. New York: St. Martin's Press, 2005.

Pipes, Richard. Russia Under the Bolshevik Regime. New York: Vintage Books, 1995.

Purkiser, W. T., Taylor, Richard S., and Taylor, Willard H. God, Man & Salvation: A Biblical Theology. Kansas City, MO: Beacon Hill Press of Kansas City, 1977.

Purkiss, Diane. The English Civil War: Papists, Gentlemen, Soldiers, and Witch-finders in the Birth of Modern Britain. New York: Basic Books, 2006.

Quarles, Benjamin. The Negro in the American Revolution. New York: W. W. Norton and Co., 1961.

_____ Black Abolitionists. New York: Oxford University Press, 1969.

Radzinsky, Edvard. The Last Tsar: The Life and Death of Nicholas II. New York: Anchor Books, 1993.

_____ Stalin: The First In-depth Biography Based on Explosive New Documents from Russia's Archives. New York: Anchor Books, 1997.

Ralph, Philip Lee., et al. World Civilizations: Their History and Their Culture, 2 vols. New York: W. W. Norton and Co., 1991.

Rayfield, Donald. Stalin and His Hangmen: The Tyrant and Those Who Killed for Him. New York: Random House, 2004.

Reed, John. Ten Days that Shook the World. New York: Penguin Books, 1977.

Rhode, Deborah L., ed. Moral Leadership: The Theory and Practice of Power, Judgment & Policy. San Francisco, CA: Jossey-Bass, 2006.

Roberts, J. A. G. The Complete History of China. Phoenix Mill, Britain: Stton Publishing, 2006.

Robertson, Geoffrey. The Tyrannicide Brief: The Story of the Man Who Sent Charles I to the Scaffold. New York: Pantheon Books, 2005.

Rodney, Walter. How Europe UnderDeveloped Africa. Washington, D.C.: Howard University Press, 1982.

Rosenthal, Franz. The Muslim Conception of Freedom Prior to the 19th Century. Leiden: E. J. Brill, 1960.

Rotberg, Robert I., ed. Rebellion in Black Africa. London: Oxford University Press, 1971.

_____ and Mazrui, Ali A., eds. Power and Protest in Black Africa. New York: Oxford University Press, 1970.

Rubenstein, Joshua and Naumou, Vladimir P., eds. Stalin's Secret

Pogrom: The Post-War Inquisition of the Jewish Anti-Fascist Committee. New Haven, CT: Yale University Press, 2005.

Rubin, Barry. Modern Dictators: Third World Coup Makers, Strongmen, and Populist Tyrants. New York: New American Library, 1987.

Schama, Simon. A History of Britain, 2 vols. New York: Hyperion, 2001.

Schechter, Betty. The Peaceable Revolution: The Story of Non-violence Resistance. Boston, MA: Houghton Mifflin Co., 1963.

Segal, Ronald. Islam's Black Slaves: The Other Black Diaspora. New York: Farrar, Straus, and Giroux, 2001.

Senge, Peter, et al. The Necessary Revolution: How Individuals and Organizations Are Working Together to Create a Sustainable World. New York: Doubleday, 2008.

Service, Robert. Stalin: A Biography. Cambridge, MA: Harvard University Press, 2004.

_____ A History of Modern Russia from Nicholas II to Vladimir Putin. Cambridge, MA: Harvard University Press, 2003.

_____ Lenin: A Biography. Cambridge, MA: Harvard University Press, 2000.

Shaughnessy, Edward L., ed. China, Empire, and Civilization. New York: Oxford University Press, 2005.

Shirazi, Imam Muhammad. War, Peace and Non-violence: An Islamic Perspective. London: Fountain Books, 2001.

Short, Philip. Mao: A Life. New York: Henry Holt and Co., 2001.

Shukman, Harold. Lenin and the Russian Revolution. Hoboken, NJ: Wiley-Blackwell, 1994.

Skinner, Tom. Words of Revolution: A Call to Involvement in the Real Revolution. Grand Rapids, MI: Zondervan, 1970.

Sklar, Richard L. Nigerian Political Parties. Princeton, NJ: Princeton University Press, 1963.

Smelser, Neil J., ed. Karl Marx on Society and Social Change With

Selections by Fredrich Engels. Chicago, IL: The University of Chicago Press, 1973.

Smith, Goldwin. A Constitutional and Legal History of England. New York: Dorset Press, 1990.

Smith, Linda T. Decolonizing Methodologies: Research and Indigenous Peoples. London: Zed Books, 1999.

Smythe, Hugh H. and Mabel M. The New Nigerian Elite. Stanford, CA: Stanford University Press, 1960.

Sole, Jacques. Questions of the French Revolution: A Historical Overview. New York: Pantheon Books, 1989.

Spence, Jonathan. Mao-Zedong: A Penguin Life. New York: Penguin, 1999.

Spence, Jonathan D. Emperor of China: Self-Portrait of K'ang hsi. New York: Vintage Books, 1988.

Spencer, Robert., ed. The Myth of Islamic Tolerance: How Islamic Law Treats Non-Muslims. Amherst, New York: Prometheus Books, 2005.

Stengel, Richard. Mandela's Way: Fifteen Lessons on Life, Love, and Courage. New York: Crown Publishers, 2009.

Suri, Jeremi. Power and Protest: Global Revolution and the Rise of Detente. Cambridge, MA: Harvard University Press, 2003.

Thompson, John M. Revolutionary Russia, 1917. New York: Charles Scribner's Sons, 1981.

_____ Leaders of the French Revolution. New York: Basil Blackwell, 1988.

Thompson, Leonard. A History of South Africa. New Haven, CT: Yale University Press, 2000.

Titus, Harold H., Smith, Marilyn S., and Nolan, Richard T. Living Issues in Philosophy. New York: D. Van Nostrand Co., 1979.

Trotsky, Leon. The Revolution Betrayed. Mineola, New York: Dover Publications, 2004.

_____ The History of the Russian Revolution. New York: Pathfinder, 2001.

Trueblood, Elton. <u>Declaration of Freedom</u>. New York: Harper and Brothers, 1955.

Trueblood, D. Elton. <u>Philosophy of Religion</u>. Grand Rapids, MI: Baker Book House, 1977.

Tutu, Desmond. <u>No Future Without Forgiveness</u>. New York: Doubleday, 1999.

Uwachue, Raph. <u>Makers of Modern Africa: Profiles in History</u>. London: Africa books Ltd., 1991.

Vallance, Edward. <u>Glorious Revolution: 1688— Britain's Fight for Liberty</u>. New York: Pegasus Books, 2007.

Ventura, Jesse. <u>Don't Start the Revolution Without Me</u>. New York: Skyhorse Publishing, 2008.

Vernadsky, George. <u>The Origins of Russia</u>. Oxford: Clarendon Press, 1959.

Waldinger, Renee; Dawson, Philip; and Woloch, Isser; ed. <u>The French Revolution and the Meaning of Citizenship</u>. Westport, CT: Greenwood Publishing Group, 1993.

Warth, Robert D. <u>Nicholas II: The Life and Reign of Russia's Last Monarch</u>. Westport, CT: Praeger, 1997.

Welty, Paul Thomas., ed. <u>African Cultures</u>. Philadelphia, PA: J. B. Lippincott Co., 1974.

Wheen, Francis. <u>Karl Marx: A Life</u>. New York: W. W. Norton and Co., 1999.

Wolfe, Bertram D. <u>Three Who Made A Revolution: Biographical History of Lenin, Trotsky and Stalin</u>. New York: Cooper Square Press, 2001.

Wood, Gordon S. <u>The Purpose of the Past: Reflections on the Uses of History</u>. New York: Penguin Books, 2008.

_____ <u>Revolutionary Characters: What Made the Founders Different</u>. New York: Penguin Books, 2006.

_____ <u>The American Revolution: A History</u>. New York: The Modern Library, 2003.

_____ The Radicalism of the American Revolution. New York: Vintage Books, 1993.

Yohannan, K. P. Revolution in World Missions. Carrollton, TX: Gospel for Asia. 2004.

Zickel, Raymond E., ed. Soviet Union: A Country Study. Washington, D.C.: Government Printing Office, 1991.

ARTICLES, THESES, AND DISSERTATIONS.

Abati, Reuben. "Laughing and Crying At Xmas." The Nigerian Guardian, December 25, 2009.

Aruna, Habib. "I'll Return to Power With Popular Mandate." Daily Independent, April 9, 2007.

Attah, Okon Effiong. "The Role of African Soldiers in Politics: New Directions in Comparing Civilian and Military Regimes." Ph.D.

diss., Washington University, St. Louis, Missouri, 1989.

Clarke, John Henrik. "The African World Revolution." cited in www.oopau.org/9.html.

Etuk, Emma S. "Hollow Promises of 'Never Again': The Genocides of Rwanda and Darfur in a Disengaged and Callous World." An unpublished Research Paper presented at Howard University dated April 4-7, 2007.

Gaido, Daniel and Walters, David. "The Progress and Problems of the African Revolution." International Socialist Review, 27, 2, Spring, 1966.

Hazzad, Ardo. "Nigeria: Muslim Pupils Kill Teacher Over Koran." cited in Naijanet.com News Headline, March 21, 2007.

Hill, Patrice. "China Becomes the Growth Engine: U. S. Dislodged As World's Pace-setter." The Washington Times, July 26, 2007.

Maxwell, George. "Problems of the African Revolution." African Communist Journal, 1, October 1959.

Olanrewaju, Sulaimon. "Condition for a Revolution in Nigeria." Nigeria Tribune, April 4, 2008.

Oliver, Roland. "The African Revolution." <u>The New York Review of Books</u>, 4, 11, July 1, 1965.

Osunde, Olu, et al. "Nigeria: A Walking Corpse." <u>Tribune</u>, December 26, 2009.

Oyerele, Kola, et al. "Bloody Day in Kano," <u>Nigerian Tribune</u>, April 18, 2007.

Rodney, Walter. "The African Revolution." <u>Urgent Tasks</u>, 12, 1981.

Torulagha, Priye Sunday. "A Study of Moral Norms Concerning War in Precolonial Traditional Nigerian Societies." Ph.D. diss., The University of Oklahoma, Norman, Oklahoma, 1990.

Zachary, G. Pascal. "The Coming Revolution in Africa." <u>The Wilson Quarterly</u>, Winter 2008.

ABOUT THE AUTHOR

Best-selling and award-winning author, international motivational speaker, and professional historian, Emma Samuel Etuk is the President of Emida International Publishers. A graduate of Howard University in Washington, D.C., he obtained a Ph.D. in United States History, with minors in African History and International Relations.

Formerly a civil servant, Etuk attended the Polytechnic, Calabar, in Nigeria, where he received a Higher National Diploma (HND) in Estate Management. He also received a B.A. degree in Business Administration from Malone College, Canton, Ohio; an M.A. in Church History from Ashland Theological Seminary; and did graduate work at the Institute of Church and State at Baylor University in Waco, Texas. At seminary, Etuk studied under Drs. David A. Rausch, Douglas Chismar, and Jerry R. Flora.

Etuk has taught history and other graduate courses at Howard, Dillard, and Morgan State universities as well as Bethune-Cookman College (now University). He has lectured in The Gambia, Nigeria and the United States. He has written and published twelve books and several articles and essays which have widely been read. Two of his books are re-published abroad and are circulating in over ten countries, including India, Pakistan, Nigeria, Malaysia, Indonesia, Sri Lanka, Nepal, Bangladesh, Bhutan, and Kenya.

Etuk is the recipient of many awards, including the 2005 Irwin Award for the Best International Campaign; the LABBE Award (2005) in recognition of his book, Recipe For Success, and the 2005

Akwa Ibom State Association of Nigeria (USA) Leadership Award in recognition of his exemplary leadership in the community.Index

He has been heard on more than 600 radio-talk shows in the USA and seen on many TV programs in Nigeria, The Gambia, and USA. He had been a member of the National Speakers Association (NSA); the Association of American Publishers (AAP); the Small Publishers Association of North America (SPAN); and the African Studies Association (ASA). He has two more manuscripts awaiting publication.

Etuk travels widely conducting workshops, seminars, and lectures on the subjects related to his books. He also speaks at Churches and on success, motivation, visionary leadership, time-management, the family, research, and the art of writing. He can be reached at emida1@ yahoo.com. This is his 13th book.

INDEX

A

A Bloody Revolution xix, 20, 23, 35, 40, 42, 43, 46, 54, 56
Abraham 33, 59, 63
absolutism 67, 73, 86, 92, 94, 95, 100, 102, 104, 105
Academic scholars 105
a Christian hope 39
actualists 6
Adedeji, Dr. Adebayo 116, 155
advocate of the traditional 30
Africa xiii, xiv, xix, xx, xxi, 5, 6, 13, 14, 15, 16, 17, 18, 19, 20, 21, 22, 23, 24, 25, 26, 27, 28, 32, 39, 42, 44, 47, 49, 50, 51, 52, 53, 58, 63, 66, 73, 74, 82, 83, 92, 94, 95, 112, 114, 115, 116, 117, 118, 119, 120, 121, 122, 123, 125, 126, 128, 130, 132, 133, 137, 142, 150, 152, 155, 156
  inevitable Revolution xxi
  needs 13, 16, 53, 63, 128
  rulers of 94
  will be free 130
African xiii, xiv, xv, xvi, xvii, xix, xx, xxi, 6, 7, 11, 13, 14, 15, 16, 17, 18, 19, 20, 22, 23, 24, 25, 26, 28, 29, 30, 31, 35, 36, 37, 38, 39, 40, 42, 45, 47, 49, 50, 51, 53, 54, 55, 56, 57, 58, 63, 66, 67, 73, 74, 77, 78, 83, 93, 94, 95, 100, 103, 104, 112, 113, 114, 115, 116, 117, 118, 119, 120, 121, 122, 123, 124, 125, 126, 127, 128, 129, 130, 131, 132, 133, 137, 138, 139, 140, 141, 143, 150, 155, 156
African American elites 16
African governments 23, 119, 120
African life xix, 6, 15, 51, 119
African Manifesto 6, 137
African Revolutionary Theology 30, 35
African Revolution, The xiv, 14, 15, 29, 58, 124, 126, 129, 132, 138, 140, 155
  meaning in this life xv
Africans do not forget 55
Africans had no choice 119
African slaves 122
African thinkers 83
African unity 16, 83
Afro-pessimism 6
Age of Absolutism, the 67
Age of Revolution, the 68, 137, 145
alternative revolution 54
American xiv, xv, xx, 2, 4, 5, 11, 15, 16, 19, 24, 25, 30, 35, 43, 45, 46, 47, 49, 52, 54, 56, 58, 73, 74, 75, 76, 77, 78, 79, 80, 81, 82, 83, 84, 86, 94, 101, 117, 126, 133, 136, 138, 142, 144, 147, 148, 149, 154
American historian 16
American Revolution xiv, 2, 4, 25, 58, 73, 74, 75, 76, 79, 80, 81, 83, 86, 136, 147, 148, 149
  the third 5, 25, 81
republican dispensation xv

the Savior 65, 66
the slave trade 115
the third American revolution 5, 25, 81
the true African revolutionaries 104
the weapons 34
the will of God 39
the word of God 37, 38
Tom Skinner 30, 31, 137, 140, 143
Toombs, L. E. 33, 34, 141
totalitarian power 10
traders 69, 114
tradition 31, 50, 61, 76, 95, 107, 127
traditional 27, 30, 31, 38, 116
tragic futility 4
transformation 5, 15, 37, 48, 103, 105, 111, 117, 119
transformation of the human soul and spirit 5
traumatic 26, 31
true African revolutionaries, the 104
trust 66, 119, 126

U

unendurable 43, 108
United Kingdom 67
universal freedom 32
U. S. President John F. Kennedy 131, 133
U. S. President Woodrow Wilson 118

V

Vernon C. Grounds 3, 4, 5, 6, 14, 15, 23, 29, 38, 56, 57, 132, 136, 137, 138, 140, 141, 143
victories 90, 92
violent 4, 5, 24, 31, 43, 46, 110, 117, 128, 131, 133
visionary ideas 16
visionary leaders 45, 60, 127

vital 6, 117

W

war 4, 5, 8, 9, 11, 12, 15, 17, 22, 23, 24, 25, 27, 28, 31, 32, 33, 34, 35, 38, 39, 42, 43, 47, 53, 54, 55, 67, 68, 69, 70, 71, 72, 74, 75, 76, 77, 78, 79, 81, 82, 83, 89, 90, 92, 95, 97, 98, 101, 105, 107, 108, 111, 115, 116, 117, 118, 122, 124, 126, 131, 140, 141, 143, 146, 147, 152, 155
warfare 4, 11, 12, 34, 111
war in heaven 8, 9, 131
warning 132, 133
war on slavery 126
Washington, George 35, 75, 76, 79
way of life 4, 46, 52
weaker nations 55
weapons, the 34
W. E. B. Du Bois 16, 155
Western ethicists 52
Western world 31, 50, 52, 53, 55, 122
whole gospel 38
wicked 10, 17, 22, 38
will of God, the 39
Wilson, Woodrow, U. S. President 118
Winston Churchill 67, 73, 145
witchcraft 28
Women xiv, 12, 18, 25, 33, 35, 37, 38, 61, 63, 69, 76, 77, 78, 83, 87, 91, 94, 98, 99, 122, 123, 126, 127, 128, 150
word of God, the 37, 38
World Revolution and Religion (1931) 4
World War II 11, 31, 55, 67, 116, 118
    hero 67